First published in 1992 by Rainbow Books,
Elsley House, 24–30 Great Titchfield Street,
London, W1P 7AD.

10 9 8 7 6 5 4 3 2 1

Originally published in 1982 by Grisewood &
Dempsey Ltd.

© Grisewood & Dempsey Ltd 1982.

ISBN 1 871745 96 9

Printed in Italy by Vallardi Industrie Grafiche.

The Vienna State Opera Ballet dances
Etudes, a ballet which tells the story of a
ballet class. It begins with learning steps and
ends with exciting movements.

my first
ENCYCLOPEDIA
IN COLOUR

Edited by John Paton

RAINBOW

In the future, people will find new ways of producing energy. This picture shows one possible way. Huge underwater turbines with blades hundreds of metres across will be turned by ocean currents to make electricity.

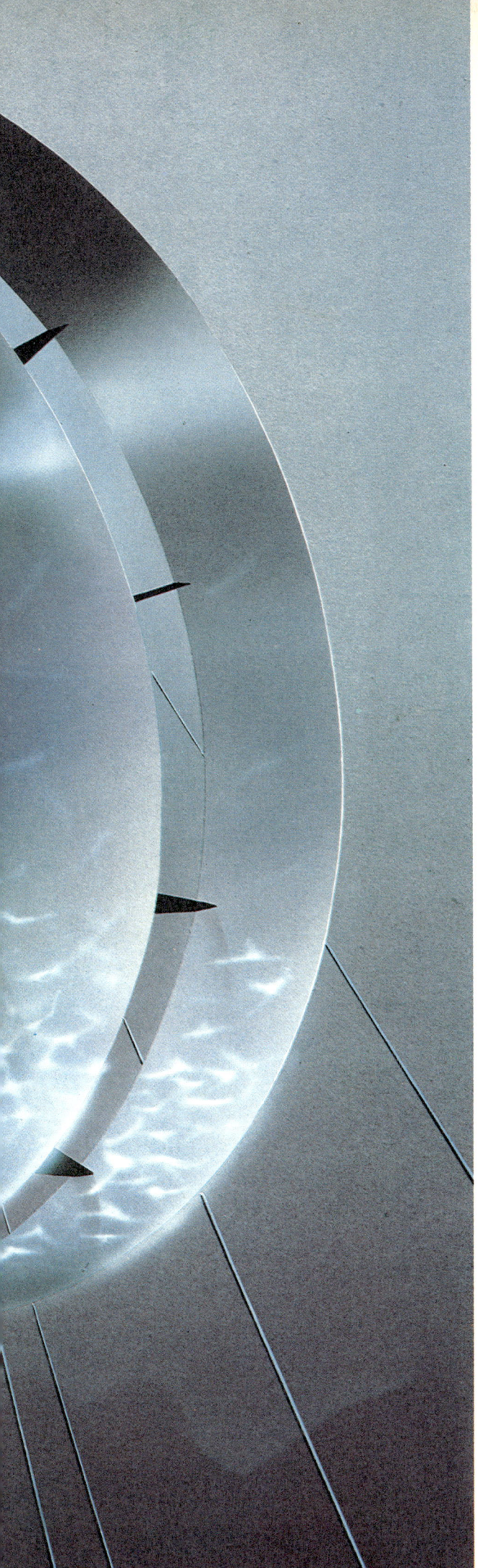

Contents

The World of Long Ago

The First People   10
Stonehenge   12
The Ancient Egyptians   14
Ancient Greece   16
Alexander the Great   18
How the Romans Lived   20
How they Lived in Ancient China   22
The Spread of Islam   24
Genghis Khan   26
The Vikings   28
The Incas   30
The Middle Ages   32
Knights and Armour   34
Inside a Perfect Castle   36
The First Ships   38
The Spanish Armada   40
The Great Days of Sail   42
Christopher Columbus   44
The Industrial Revoluton   46
Early Railways   48

The World of Nature

Dinosaurs   52
All About Shells   54
The Great Apes   56
The Fastest Animals   58
Animal Homes   60
Birds   62
Insects   64
All About Dogs   66
Horses and Ponies   68
Cats of all Kinds   70
Animals with Pouches   72
The Busy Beaver   74
Trees   76
Wild Flowers   78
Fire from the Earth   80

The World of Science

The Fiery Sun   84
The Sun's Family   86
Our Planet Earth   88
Our Moon   90
Under the Sea   92
Why Things Fall   94
The Power of Steam   96
Simple Machines   98
All Kinds of Sounds   100
Inside a Big Aircraft   102
The Story of the Tank   104
The Future   106

The World of Art

An Ancient Greek Theatre   110
Buildings, Old and New   112
The Renaissance   114
Three Famous Painters   116
Ballet   118
Three Famous Composers   120
The Crafts   122

The World of
LONG AGO

The First People

Man is the only creature to discover how to make fire. Fire gave the first men light, warmth and safety from prowling enemies.

The first people probably looked like those in the picture. They lived in Africa about 2 million years ago. All that remains of them today is a few bones found in the soil. But from these bones scientists can build up a picture of these first people and how they lived.

From Apes To Men

Our earliest ancestors were ape-like creatures. They lived in the forests and ran on all fours. Over many millions of years these animals changed. They moved down from the trees and hunted for food on the open plains. They began to walk upright on their back legs. This meant their front legs, or arms, were free to make and carry things.

The ape-men had many enemies. They had no claws or teeth to use as weapons against wild animals. Instead, they relied on their wits. Their brains were bigger than those of other animals, so they were cleverer. They learned to live together in groups, for safety. They learned how to talk and how to make simple tools.

Their lives were very hard. They had no homes but wandered in search of food. They ate seeds, nuts, berries and roots. When they killed an animal, they ate the meat raw, for they did not know how to make fire.

These are some early stone tools. The first men picked up stones that were roughly the right shape. Then they chipped away flakes to make a cutting tool. Later, stones were shaped very skilfully to make all kinds of tools.

People Like Us

About a million years ago, ape-men had given way to people who looked more like us. They knew how to make fire. With fire, people could scare away fierce animals, cook food and keep warm.

Life was still very hard. Some people lived in caves. On the rock walls they drew pictures of the animals they hunted.

Clothes and Weapons

Man's first tools were made from pebbles. Stones were chipped to make a cutting edge. Later, hunters made spears tipped with sharp flints. They made clothes from animal skins and wore ornaments of bones and teeth.

People still had no settled homes. They followed the herds of animals they hunted for food. Only when people discovered how to plant crops, did settled village life begin.

This is a cave painting of a spotted horse. The outline of the horse has been drawn in black on a background of painted rock. Above the horse, the cave painter has left a print of his hand. This painting was found inside a cave in France. There are other cave paintings in Spain.

This is how the primitive ape-men may have lived. The hunters have killed an antelope. Now they drive away hungry hyenas and jackals who want to steal the food. The cave gives shelter from wind and rain, and from enemies such as leopards. These people do not know how to make fire, so they will eat the meat raw. They also eat leaves, fruit and berries, and dig for roots. They wear no clothes. But they use simple stone tools. See the woman using a stone to break open a bone to get at the juicy marrow. They have inquisitive minds. So even a stick is turned to good use.

11

Stonehenge

On Salisbury Plain in southern England stands a mysterious circle of great standing stones. This is Stonehenge. It was built between 3000 and 1500 BC. But we do not know much about the people who built it

The Mystery of Stonehenge

No-one really knows what Stonehenge was built for. It may have been some kind of temple. We know that the stones were set up very carefully, to match the positions of the Sun and Moon at different times of the year. Perhaps Stonehenge was a giant calendar. Stones for Stonehenge were brought more than 300 kilometres from the mountains of South Wales.

An ancient stone tomb. It is made from great stones or "megaliths". Stone tombs and monuments were made by the people living in western Europe from about 4000 BC.

The builders of Stonehenge had to drag the huge stones long distances. When the stones reached the site, they had to be raised carefully into position. Ropes and poles were used to tilt the stones into the holes. The cross stones were raised up on platforms until they could be fitted into place on top of the standing stones.

The Ancient Egyptians

More than 5000 years ago, people settled along the banks of the River Nile in Egypt. Either side of the river lay hot, dry desert. But along the river banks, the land was rich and fertile. In the green valley of the Nile arose the great civilization of ancient Egypt.

People of the Nile

The Nile was very important to the Egyptians. Every year the water rose, flooding the fields. After the floods went down the farmers could plant their crops in the rich soil. They dug canals to store water to feed the crops during the long dry months ahead.

The Egyptians grew corn and fruit. They kept cattle and poultry. They hunted and fished along the Nile. Boats carried goods up and down the river. Egyptian ladies used make-up, and everyone enjoyed music and games. Rich people lived in fine houses with beautiful gardens. Meanwhile, in the hot desert thousands of slaves were toiling to build enormous pyramids.

The Egyptians were skilled craftsmen. This is a black granite statue of a king called Senuseret III. He must have been an unhappy man, for he is always shown with a sad face.

Below we see how a great pyramid must have looked during building work. The heavy stones were dragged into place on sledges. Hundreds of slaves were needed to pull them up the long ramps. Other slaves are sharpening tools for the expert stone masons who did the finishing work. Nearby the master builders in charge of the work are looking at their plans which are drawn on papyrus scrolls.

Tomb of the Pharaohs

The kings of Egypt were known as pharaohs. When a king died, he was buried in a tomb deep beneath a huge stone pyramid. You can still see pyramids in Egypt today. The most famous ones are at Giza and the largest was built for the pharaoh Khufu.

The Egyptians believed in life after death. So a dead person was buried with the things he would need in the next world, such as clothes, furniture and jewels. The body was treated with special substances to stop decay and wrapped in bandages. We call this preserved body a "mummy". After the mummy was buried, the tomb was shut tight to keep out robbers.

Treasures of the King

Later, the Egyptians buried their pharaohs in a secret valley called the Valley of the Kings. Even here robbers broke into the tombs to steal the treasures inside. Only one small tomb escaped. It contained the mummy of the boy-king Tutankhamen. In 1922 it was found and opened. Inside was a wonderful treasure.

From the early "step" pyramids (top) the Egyptians moved on to build the great pyramids at Giza (above). The centre pyramid, that of Khafre, still has some of its original limestone outer skin.

This small stone frog was carved in Egypt about 3000 BC.

The Egyptians used a form of picture writing called hieroglyphics. For paper they used a kind of parchment made from the papyrus reed. They were among the first peoples to use a system of writing.

Ancient Greece

At the height of its power (from 443 to 429 BC), Athens was the greatest of all Greek cities. For hundreds of years it was probably the most splendid city in the world. Here great teachers and thinkers, such as Plato and Aristotle, taught. People watched plays in the great open-air theatres.

Greek art and architecture are admired to this day, and the Greeks' love of athletics led to the start of the Olympic Games.

Yet, for all its beauty, Athens was not a free city. It depended on the toil and sweat of thousands of slaves. Most of these slaves were captured when Greek armies conquered other states.

Everyday Life in Ancient Greece

Women – both freeborn and slaves – spent most of the day at home. The mistress of the house set her slaves to work at the household tasks, and helped with such crafts as spinning and weaving. She looked after the children and also managed the family's money. But her husband did not expect her to do anything outside the house. He even saw to the family shopping.

Leaving the house at dawn, the husband spent the day in the town, at work, chatting with friends, exercising at the gymnasium, or perhaps going hunting – a favourite pastime. He did not usually return home until the evening, in time for dinner.

Boys were sent to school after their sixth birthday. But girls stayed at home, to be taught by their mother or by slaves. Boys left school at 15. At 18 an Athenian boy became a citizen and promised to defend his country and obey its laws.

1. Temple offices. 2. Propylaeum or gateway. 3. Statue of Athena. 4. The Parthenon, most important of all the temples. 5. Great altar of Athena. 6. Sanctuary of Zeus. 7. The Erectheion, which today houses the oldest known image of Athena.

Boy and girl slaves. Most slaves were captured in war and sold in the market. They did all kinds of jobs, includng cooking, street-cleaning and even teaching! Some house slaves lived as members of a family and earned enough money to buy their freedom. But most slaves had hard lives.

The Greeks liked loose, comfortable clothes. Both men and women wore the tunic-like chiton (2 and 4). Over it, they draped a woollen outer garment called a himation. The peplos (1 and 3) was pinned at the shoulder by a brooch and worn with a belt.

1   2   3   4

The Greeks loved games and sports. This relief sculpture shows a boy rolling a hoop. The hoops were made of iron, and some had bells fixed to them.

The Acropolis at Athens

Athens is the capital of modern Greece. In ancient times, it grew from a small town to a powerful city-state. Its crowning jewel was the Acropolis, a holy place with many beautiful temples.

The Acropolis was once a hill fort. The city grew around the fort. There was only one pathway up the rocky hillside to the Acropolis and only one gateway. The goddess Athena watched over Athens and gave the city her name. The Parthenon, the most impressive of all the temples, was her temple. Zeus, the king of the gods, was not forgotten, but he had to be content with a much smaller sanctuary.

The picture shows the Athens Acropolis as it looked at the height of its glory. Today, many of its buildings are in ruins but people from all over the world are still eager to see what remains of one of the true wonders of the ancient world.

Alexander the Great

Alexander the Great lived more than two thousand years ago. He is still remembered today because he was a clever and powerful king, and one of the best leaders the world has ever known. By the time he died, the empire he had conquered was larger than any other before him, or since.

Below: Alexander's horse, Bucephalus, was almost as famous as its rider! Alexander brought his horse with him from Macedonia, and used it in battle for many years. When Bucephalus died in India, Alexander named a new city in its honour.

Right: Alexander the Great's empire is all the land inside the black line. Although he fought many battles he was a just ruler over the lands he conquered, and rewarded loyalty with kindness and respect. When he died, his generals divided the empire amongst themselves.

GREECE

ASIA MINOR

SYRIA

Mediterranean Sea

PERSIA

EGYPT

River Nile

River Indus

Border of Alexander's empire

The Macedonian King

Alexander began as king of a small country called Macedonia, to the north of Greece. His father, King Phillip, had planned to take an army to Asia. Greek people there had been taken over by the Persian king, and Phillip wanted to free them. When Phillip died, Alexander took the army instead.

Alexander was only 20 years old, but his army trusted him and he led them well. Soon he had won back the Greek cities, but he did not return to Macedonia. Instead, he took his army further east. They won every battle they fought, and the Persian king's empire was no longer safe. The Persian army was much bigger than Alexander's, but the leaders were not so clever.

Persia and Egypt

Next, Alexander went to Egypt. He conquered all the cities there, and was made Pharaoh. A new Egyptian city was named Alexandria after him. Then he returned to Persia. The king was waiting for him, and fought a great battle. But Alexander's army won the battle, and now Alexander was the king of Persia as well.

East to India

But Alexander did not stop there. His army now was enormous, for many of the people he had conquered joined his troops. They now all travelled further east, across the plains to India. In those days, people thought that the Earth was smaller than it is. They thought that the land ended on the other side of India, and Alexander wanted to go to the edge of the world.

But when the army reached India, his soldiers were tired of war. They wanted to go back home to their families. So Alexander agreed to turn back. They returned to Persia, building new cities along the way.

Everywhere the army went, they brought Greek ideas and Greek buildings with them. The new cities were run along Greek lines. Alexander's empire meant that thousands of people's lives were changed for ever.

The End in Babylon

Alexander never returned to Macedonia. He died in the Persian city of Babylon, at the age of 32. But the effects of his short life lasted for hundreds of years in the new countries he made.

How the Romans Lived

This fine Roman town house has an opening in the roof called a compluvium. This let light and air into the central part of the house. The picture also shows you what other rooms in the house were like.

tablinum

atrium

impluvium

Wealthy Romans liked privacy. So the house has high walls, with no windows. On one side, the outer rooms have been let off as shops.

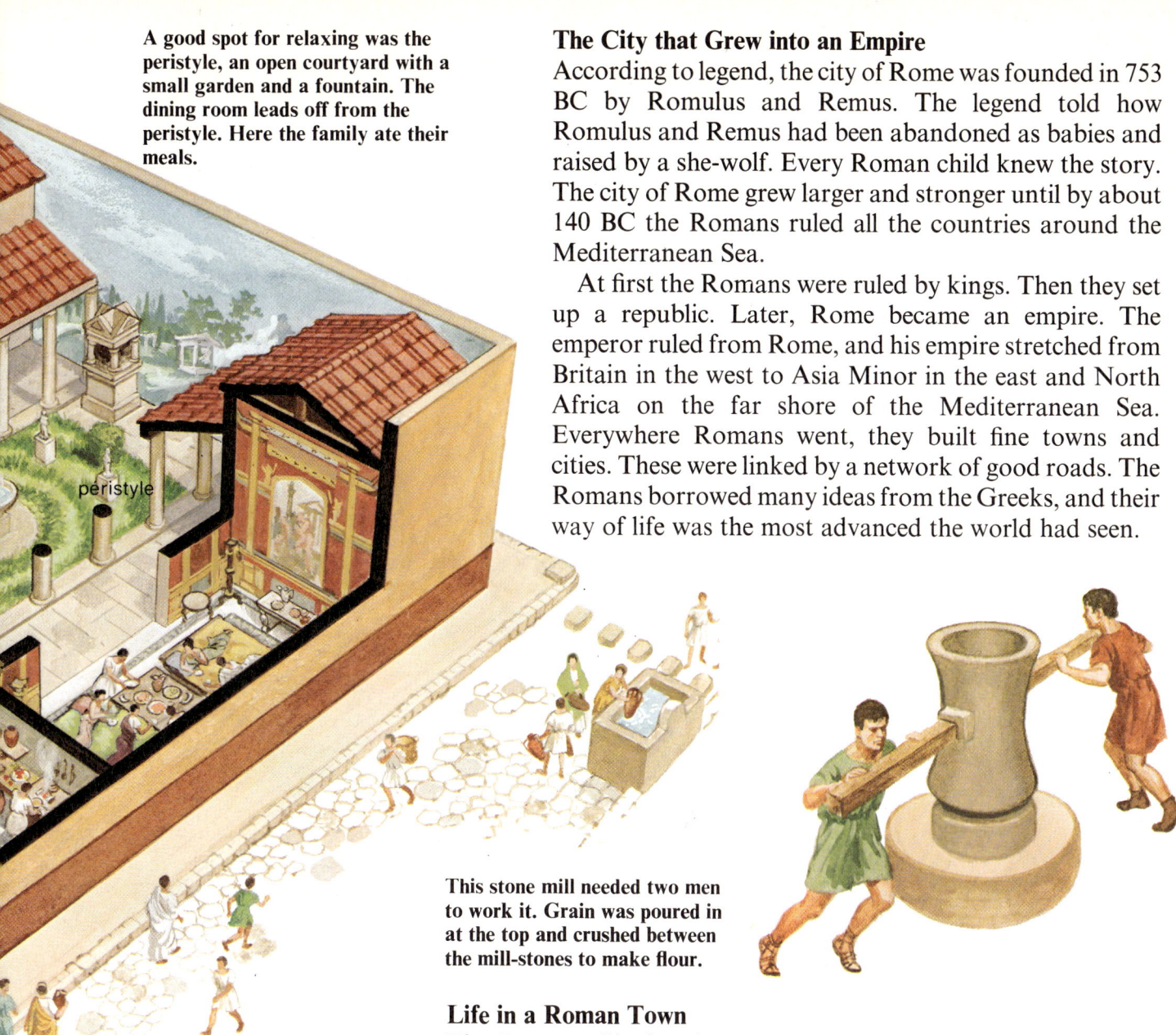

A good spot for relaxing was the peristyle, an open courtyard with a small garden and a fountain. The dining room leads off from the peristyle. Here the family ate their meals.

peristyle

Only a rich Roman could afford a fine house like this. Visitors enter the house through a narrow passage leading to the atrium. In the centre of the atrium is a pool called the impluvium. Here rainwater is collected, for the atrium is open to the sky.

Guests are entertained in a reception room called the tablinum. On the ground floor are bedrooms, storerooms, the kitchen and the lavatory. Upstairs are more bedrooms and the slaves' rooms. There is no bathroom, since Romans preferred to bathe at the public baths. Drinking water comes from a trough in the street.

The City that Grew into an Empire

According to legend, the city of Rome was founded in 753 BC by Romulus and Remus. The legend told how Romulus and Remus had been abandoned as babies and raised by a she-wolf. Every Roman child knew the story. The city of Rome grew larger and stronger until by about 140 BC the Romans ruled all the countries around the Mediterranean Sea.

At first the Romans were ruled by kings. Then they set up a republic. Later, Rome became an empire. The emperor ruled from Rome, and his empire stretched from Britain in the west to Asia Minor in the east and North Africa on the far shore of the Mediterranean Sea. Everywhere Romans went, they built fine towns and cities. These were linked by a network of good roads. The Romans borrowed many ideas from the Greeks, and their way of life was the most advanced the world had seen.

This stone mill needed two men to work it. Grain was poured in at the top and crushed between the mill-stones to make flour.

Life in a Roman Town

The Romans liked order. Their towns were laid out rather like chessboards. Streets made a regular pattern. In the larger squares were important public buildings, such as the forum or meeting place, the theatre, and the temple. Other squares were made up of private houses and shops.

A Roman town was like an "island" of civilization. Inside the strong walls, the townsfolk felt safe from enemies. People came to the town from country villages to sell goods, to pay taxes, and perhaps to watch gladiators fight in the arena. Roman towns amazed visitors from other lands, who had never seen houses with central heating and running water.

The Romans at Home

The house in the picture belongs to a rich Roman family. They have slaves to clean and cook for them. Wealthy Romans entertained guests at banquets that lasted for hours. Favourite foods were chicken and other birds, fish, roast meat basted with honey, vegetables and fruit, washed down with wine. People ate with their fingers, lying on couches beside the table.

How they Lived in Ancient China

Over 2000 years ago, when most of Europe was still a collection of warring tribes, China already had a very advanced civilization. In its great cities merchants traded goods from all over the East and rich officials and nobles lived in splendid fashion.

Work on the Land

Most of the people in ancient China were poor farmers. They worked their land to keep their families and pay their taxes. If a farmer had a drought, flood or poor harvest, he often had to sell everything to pay his taxes. Then he had no choice but to work for someone else. Each year every man between the ages of 23 and 56 had to spend one

month working for the emperor. He might help dig canals, work in an iron or salt mine, or even work on the Great Wall itself, built to keep out invaders.

Life for the Rich

In the cities, the poor lived in small, cramped shacks made of mud and straw. But many people in cities grew rich from trade or taxes. Very rich people might live in houses with three or four storeys and many courtyards. The courtyards contained beautiful willows and pine trees and fishponds full of golden carp.

The house of an important official (shown above) was not so grand, but even so it was

Left: The house of a rich man in ancient China. The wooden pillars and beams in the main part of the house were gaily painted and lacquered. The walls were plaster, painted with geometric designs. We know the type of houses people lived in from models and pictures found in tombs of this period.

surrounded by a wall for privacy and protection. Two courtyards separated the house from the main gate. From a watchtower built into one of the walls a guard kept a constant lookout for intruders. The rooms of the house were built around the inner courtyard. There were bedrooms and two private sitting rooms, a large one for the master and a smaller one for his wife. There was also a banqueting hall, richly decorated with silk hangings, painted screens and bronze urns full of dried flowers. The guests sat on the floor on fur rugs, mats and colourful cushions.

Poor people in the cities lived in small, cramped shacks like this one. The walls were made of dried mud and the roof was thatched. There was little protection from the winter cold.

The Market-place

The centre of a busy town was the market-place. Here goods were bought and sold. Merchants were looked down upon by many Chinese. They were thought inferior even to poor farmers, because they made money off other people and not from the land. Merchants were forbidden to take official posts and to wear silk clothes.

Also part of the market-place were the public scribes, who wrote letters and documents for people who could not write; and the soup-seller, who passed on news and gossip as he travelled from town to town.

A busy market-place in an ancient Chinese town. Near the entrance stand two officials, who supervised the trading and collected taxes from the stall-holders. All kinds of goods were sold from the stalls – fruit and vegetables, cooked meats, pots and pans, and fine cloth and jewellery.

The Spread of Islam

Left: The citadel at Aleppo in Syria, one of the strongest fortresses in the Islamic empire. This part was built by Ghazi, son of Saladin, a great Muslim battle leader of the 1100s.

Below: When the Muslims conquered Palestine, they also captured the Holy Land around Jerusalem. The Christian kings and princes of Europe began great campaigns against the Muslims, called Crusades. They wanted to capture the Holy Land back from its Arab rulers, but they were only successful for short periods. Just before 1300 the Christians were finally driven out of the Holy Land. In this picture of a battle between Muslims and Crusaders, the Crusaders are wearing the sign of the Cross.

Muslim Warfare

Most Muslim warriors rode camels or horses. Their favourite weapons were lances, swords and bows and arrows. Like Crusaders, they often wore metal helmets and shirts of *mail* (metal links). The warriors often won battles by pretending to be beaten, and riding away. Then, when the enemy soldiers relaxed, the Muslims turned on them with a deadly surprise attack.

The Arabs quickly learned how to capture enemy towns by watching how their Byzantine and Persian enemies did it. They learned to knock down walls with battering rams. They hurled stones from huge catapults. They probably forced enemy prisoners to build war machines for them. Wooden towers were made that reached the top of the enemy's walls. With soldiers inside, they were pushed up to the walls and the Muslims jumped across.

The Muslims also learned about fighting at sea from the Byzantines. They built huge wooden ships rowed by a hundred or more oarsmen. They copied the Byzantines' use of naphtha, a substance thrown at enemy ships and buildings to set them on fire. Burning naphtha was very difficult to put out. If it landed on people, it caused terrible burns.

In the 600s AD the prophet Muhammad began to preach a new religion – the religion of Islam. Muslims, as his followers are called, believe in one God, Allah. They believe that Allah rewards those faithful to him and punishes the wicked. After Muhammad's death in AD 632, his followers believed that they must spread his message outside Arabia. Islam had to conquer the world.

Conquering an Empire

Within ten years the Muslim armies had swept north through the mainly Christian Byzantine empire, including Syria, Palestine and Egypt, and west into North Africa. Iraq, Persia, and Afghanistan were next to fall. By the early 700s, the Islamic empire stretched from Spain in the west to the borders of India in the east.

Muslim Rule

The Muslim empire was ruled by leaders called caliphs. Arabic was the empire's main language. The caliphs treated most of their new subjects well, though most of the money they took in taxes went toward the caliph's splendid court. Muslims borrowed many of the best ideas of the peoples they conquered. The civilization of Islam was a mixture of ideas from many lands. Later, Europeans borrowed ideas from the Islamic world – the Arabic system of numerals, for example. Today, though the caliphs are long gone, the "Arab world", as we call it, still covers much of the original Islamic empire.

Above: Music and dance at the wedding of a powerful Muslim in India in the 1400s. Muhammad was thought to have disapproved of musical instruments, saying they were the devil's call to worship. But many people became skilled musicians and music was a part of festivals and other special occasions.

Genghis Khan

More than 800 years ago, tribes of wandering nomads lived on the plains, or steppes, of central Asia. They were called Mongols. Mongols looked rather like North American Indians. They were tough and strong and were expert riders. They had to be, for they spent days in the saddle, driving their herds to new grazing places. Mongolian winters were freezing, the summers were sweltering. The tribes often fought one another. Each wanted the best land for its herds.

The Boy Temujin

The greatest of all the Mongol leaders was Genghis Khan. He was born about 1162, the son of the chief of the Kiyat Mongols. His boyhood name was "Temujin", which means "finest steel". When he was nine years old Temujin became betrothed to the daughter of a neighbouring chief. He was taken to live in her village.

Four years later Temujin returned home to find that his father had been killed. None· of the warriors wanted to follow the young Temujin, and for a while he and his family were alone. But little by little he forced his warriors to rejoin him. Finally the day came when he could ride to claim his bride. Temujin was now a man and his tribe was strong again.

Ruler of Asia

Temujin and his warriors were soon feared by the other Mongol tribes. In 1206 the

Genghis Khan's army was trained to use speed and surprise. Often the Mongols chased an enemy so fast that they were inside a city before the gates could be shut.

Each warrior had five horses. He would ride a horse hard for one day, then let it rest for four. His horse would come to his call, like a dog.

Genghis's grandson Kublai moved the Mongol capital to Peking, in China. There he built the magnificent "Forbidden City". Marco Polo, the famous Italian traveller, visited Kublai's splendid court in Peking. He stayed with the Khan for 17 years, and travelled to many parts of the East on missions for Kublai. After the death of Kublai Khan, the Mongol empire began to break up.

tribes met and chose Temujin as their leader. They gave him a new name: Genghis Khan, Ruler of the World. Genghis was cruel to his enemies, but he rewarded loyal and honest men. Soon his armies marched into China. They swept through the countryside, leaving the cities burning behind them. Most prisoners were killed. By 1217 all of China was ruled by Genghis Khan. His empire grew until it stretched from China in the east to Persia in the west. The Mongols set up roads, collected taxes and encouraged trading.

Death of the Khan

Genghis Khan died in 1277. Under his son Ogadai and his grandson Kublai the empire grew rich. But after Kublai's death, the Mongol leaders quarrelled. Slowly, the Mongol empire broke up.

Today Mongolia is a Communist country. But there are still Mongols who ride with their herds. And they still tell stories about their greatest leader – Genghis Khan.

The Vikings

The Vikings came from Scandinavia, from the countries we now know as Norway, Sweden and Denmark. They were sailors and warriors, who ventured over the seas in their longships. The sight of a Viking ship approaching struck terror into the hearts of people all along the coasts of Europe.

Viking Ships

Viking ships were strong and seaworthy. They had a single square sail. When there was not enough wind, the crew took to the oars. The ship was steered with a rudder-oar at the stern, fixed on the right-hand side. The captain was the steersman. He kept in sight of land as much as possible. In the open sea he steered by the Sun or stars.

The Vikings were brave seamen. They made long voyages across the stormy Atlantic Ocean in search of new lands.

In 986 a Viking called Eric the Red sailed from Iceland to Greenland. He founded a settlement. "Greenland" sounded a more inviting name, especially to people coming from Iceland.

However, Greenland proved cold and barren. Eric's son Leif decided to look for somewhere warmer and greener. He sailed west, and around the year 1000 he landed in a place he called "Vinland" (Wineland). He was the first European to set foot in America.

The Vikings never managed to settle in Vinland. But they remained in Greenland for 500 years.

Raiding and Settling

At first, the Vikings were just raiders. They sailed to other lands, robbed and burned, then sailed away. Viking bands reached Russia and even explored the Mediterranean Sea. There were many Viking raids on Britain and northern France. Vikings settled in Iceland and Greenland.

Later, instead of just raiding, the Vikings went in search of new lands to settle. Whole families set off in open boats like the one in the picture. With them they took their farm animals. They tried to make the journey in stages, landing at night to rest and cook hot food.

Even so, the voyage must have been uncomfortable and dangerous. Viking ships like these sailed right across the Atlantic and reached North America.

These are the kinds of clothes the Vikings wore. Cloth was made from wool and flax. Both men and women wore metal brooches and other ornaments.

The Viking Life

Apart from being fierce fighters, the Vikings were also skilled craftsmen in wood and metal. They loved to tell stories, or "sagas", about the adventures of brave warriors.

A Viking king or chief was richly dressed. He rewarded his followers with gifts of jewels or clothes.

The Viking Gods

The chief Viking god was called Odin. His son was Thor, who carried a hammer and fought battles against evil giants.

A Viking warrior believed that if he died in battle, his spirit would be carried to the great hall of Valhalla to feast with Odin. So he was never afraid of death.

29

The Incas

The Incas were a South American people who built up a great empire between 1200 and 1300 AD. The Inca empire stretched for thousands of miles along the Andes mountains in the country we now call Peru.

Soldiers and Supplies

There were two main highways which ran from north to south of the Inca Empire. One followed the line of the coast, and the other ran through the mountains. Other smaller roads were built across country to link the two highways, while small paths branched off these to link them with all the towns and villages. The roads were very useful for moving the armies quickly and easily around the country, and many roads were built for this reason, just as the Romans built their roads. But many ordinary people used the roads as well, to take food, animals and other supplies from town to town.

Building the Roads

Most of the roads were long, and usually paved or cobbled. The valley roads were straight, but those in the mountains wound up and down very steep slopes. Sometimes steps were cut into the mountains to make the road easier to walk. Bridges and causeways were built across difficult parts, such as rivers and marshes. The Incas also built special suspension bridges across deep gorges, like the one in the background of the picture.

Help for Travellers

There were rest houses, called *tambos*, built along the roads at a day's travelling distance from one another. Here, travellers on official government business could stay the night before continuing their journeys.

The Middle Ages

The time in history that is called the Middle Ages lasted for more than a thousand years. During that time the countries of Europe were often at war, and several famous *plagues* in which many people died from diseases also happened then. But many other changes occured which, in the end, improved the lives of most people.

For much of the time, people lived under a way of government called *feudalism*. At the top of the government was the king and his nobles. They owned all the land, and rented it to knights who in turn rented it to the peasants. Most peasants were no better than slaves. They had to do exactly what they were told, and had no rights or laws to protect them from cruel masters. Their lives were often very hard and miserable.

But a new group of people developed towards the end of the Middle Ages. They were merchants, who lived by trading goods around the countries of Europe and the East. As they grew rich and powerful, towns and cities grew up along their journey routes. New skills and trades were needed to supply the towns.

The merchants' power grew so fast that the old ways of doing things, and the feudal way of government, was no longer enough. Farming was still important, but many peasants left the land and found new ways of life.

Top: This farming picture comes from a book made in the fifteenth century. It shows what peasant life was like in Europe at that time. The horse-collar in the picture was a great improvement in farming, because it meant that horses instead of oxen could be used in the fields. Oxen were much slower than horses.

Right: Religion was a very important part of everyday life in the Middle Ages. Churches and cathedrals were built all over Europe during those times, as a sign of the trust of the people in God.

The Church and the Monasteries

The Church was very powerful throughout the whole of the Middle Ages, and its power could be seen in many different ways. Large communities of men called *monks* were common at this time. The monks were religious men who lived together in monasteries. The monks were often kind and helpful to poor people, ran hospitals and orphanages, and spent a lot of time in prayer.

But the monasteries were very important in another way, too. At this time almost no-one in ordinary life could read or write, and printed books had not yet been invented. All the education and learning that existed then went on in monasteries. The knowledge from past times had to be recorded by hand in manuscripts, and the monks had special rooms in which they worked. Many of the manuscripts are illustrated with beautiful paintings.

Church Buildings

The picture on this page shows a cathedral being built in the Middle Ages. People in those days took their religion very seriously, and everyone went to church regularly, and did what the church leaders told them was right. It took many years to build a cathedral like this one, for everything had to be done by hand. The stone had to be brought to the site, and then raised into place and carefully carved. The men who did the carving, called stone *masons*, were skilful and their work was very valuable. Many of the buildings they made can still be seen today in the countries of Europe.

Knights and Armour

Armour was used in battles for thousands of years. The fighting men who wore it needed to protect their bodies against damage from the weapons of their enemies. But the sort of armour that was worn changed during the years, and was different from country to country.

Early Armour

The first armour was probably no more than a thick leather coat which covered the person's body from their neck to their thighs. The leather would have protected the wearer from some sword or spear blows, but it would not have been much good against direct hits. Later on, tiny pieces of iron or steel were sewn on to the coats to make them stronger. The coats of mail in the picture below were a better idea. Thousands of metal rings were linked together to make these.

Helmets and Shields

Cone-shaped helmets with a metal nose-piece were used a lot. The smooth metal made weapons slide off the surface and away from a direct hit. Many helmets had sheets of chain mail attached to their sides, to protect the neck as well.

Soldiers carried a sword or spear in one hand, and a shield in the other. Round shields were light and useful, but a longer one was best for a mounted soldier. It protected more of his body on his unarmed side. The extra weight did not matter so much to a man on horseback. But as body armour improved, shields got smaller again. The body armour did the job of the shield quite well, by itself.

Plate armour about 1500

Norman

Saracen

Crusader

13th century helmet

Left: The plate armour was very heavy to wear, and expensive to make. It was excellent protection, but it could only be worn by the knights who fought on horseback.

Key: 1 visor
2 breastplate
3 gauntlet
4 couter
5 cuisse
6 greave
7 sabaton

Knights and Tournaments

Tournaments were a display of fighting in peacetime, when two knights fought on horseback. They galloped at full speed until they met, and then each tried to knock the other off their horse. Although a tournament was not real fighting, it was still a very dangerous sport. Many knights were killed in tournaments instead of on the battlefield.

The knights in the picture are using only their lances on each other. The next stage of the tournament was a hand-to-hand fight on foot. The knights used battle axes, swords and maces for that part of the display.

Below: You can see that horses, as well as their riders, often wore armour into battle – even in a tournament. The horses were specially trained for their work

The tents in the background fly the flags of the different knights taking part. The knights also wear their own colours in the ribbons on their helmets.

Inside a Perfect Castle

In the Middle Ages, kings built castles to defend their lands. When a king wanted to show how strong he was, he built castles. Edward I of England did this after his army conquered Wales.

The First Castles
Early castles were simple wooden forts. From them developed the "motte-and-bailey" castle. The motte was a mound. The bailey was the area round about, protected by a wall. In the middle was the *keep*, a great stone tower. The outer walls were guarded by small towers and circled by a ditch or *moat* filled with water.

The Concentric Castle
In the late 13th and early 14th centuries, the *concentric* castle appeared. It had a lower outer wall, outside the main wall. There was no keep and no weak spot, for every part of the defence was protected by another part. The crusaders probably brought the idea of this kind of castle back to Europe from the Middle East.

The picture shows how Beaumaris Castle in Wales would have looked if Edward I had ever finished building it. Four tall round towers guard the corners of the inner bailey, and two massive D-shaped towers stand behind the two strong gatehouses. The plan of Beaumaris Castle was carefully drawn so that each tower on the outer wall is matched by its fellow on the opposite side.

From the safety of this *embrasure* or splayed opening, the archer can fire at an enemy through the narrow loophole. While he fires his crossbow, a lad or varlet loads a second bow for him so he can keep up a rapid rate of fire.

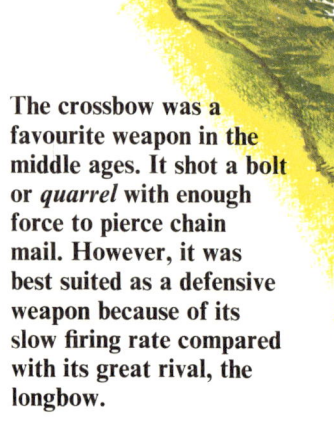

The crossbow was a favourite weapon in the middle ages. It shot a bolt or *quarrel* with enough force to pierce chain mail. However, it was best suited as a defensive weapon because of its slow firing rate compared with its great rival, the longbow.

Holding off an Attack

The defenders inside a motte-and-bailey castle could only hold out and hope that help would arrive. When an army laid siege to a castle, shortage of food and water sometimes forced the defenders to give in.

Later castles were so strong that the defenders had more chance to counter-attack. They could fire from the shelter of overhanging *hoardings* and *machiolations*. The gateways, protected by portcullises, drawbridges and an extra outwork or *barbican*, could be used to make surprise attacks or *sallies*. Sometimes the defenders would rush out through a small gate called a *sally-port* to catch the enemy unawares.

The spiral stairs wind upwards to the right. Only the defender (top) can swing his sword freely.

DAN ESCOT

The First Ships

The men who sailed the ships of the ancient world were also their own designers and ship-builders. They were always trying to make their ships bigger and better, and to sail further to other lands.

Above: The Norwegian explorer, Thor Heyerdahl, built a boat from Egyptian papyrus reeds. He sailed it across the Atlantic to prove that the Egyptians could have sailed to South America in ancient times.

The ships on these two pages are just some of the very early ways people found to travel on the water. They are all more complicated than the very first boats. The first boat would have been no more than a dug-out log, with a branch as a paddle. Sails were an important invention.

Above: Greek triremes were long, fast ships. The oars were arranged in three rows, one above the other, for extra speed in the water.

Mediterranean Ships

The ships of the Mediterranean Sea were developed in many different ways. The most famous sailors there were the Greeks, the Phoenicians and the Egyptians. These people developed ships so that they could trade with the other countries around the edge of the Mediterranean. They built different sorts of ships for trading and for fighting battles. Their ships might look rather rough to us, but they worked so well the Phoenicians even sailed as far as Britain. Their ships used rowers, but they also had sails for extra speed. The rowers were very important. Some ships had the rowers and their oars banked up in lines of two or three.

Keels and Sails

The Vikings of Scandinavia were also very famous early sailing people. They got as far as North America in their ships which were long, fast and very reliable. The Viking ships were famous for an invention which made them safe in heavy seas – the *keel*. A keel is attached to the bottom of a ship, and helps to keep it steady in the water. It also makes a ship stronger, and less likely to break up and sink.

The shape of a sail is an important part of the design of a ship. The sails in the pictures on these pages have square or rectangular sails, but the Arabs invented a different, triangular one called a *lateen*. A lateen sail was better for sailing in high winds, because it could be angled into the wind without making the ship capsize. The ships could have just one huge lateen sail, instead of two or three small square ones.

Above: A Roman round ship, built to carry goods such as grain around the Mediterranean Sea. The small sail in the bow was called an *artemon*. It made the ship easier to steer in a high wind.

Below: This ancient Egyptian boat had a mast and sail as well as oars and rowers. The small oars in the stern were used to steer. It would not have been very safe in a storm, but it was useful for short trips close to the land.

The Spanish Armada

In the 1400s, explorers from Europe charted routes to the Far East and to America. When Queen Elizabeth came to the English throne in 1558, Spain, France, the Netherlands and England were all laying claim to colonies in distant lands. It was important to have a strong navy.

Drake the Devil
Spanish galleons brought back the riches of the Americas to Spain. English sea captains such as

Francis Drake were prepared to fight the Spanish ships to win their share of the treasures of the New World. Spaniards called Drake "the Devil".

The Spanish king, Philip II, decided to invade England. He also hoped to make Protestant England Roman Catholic again. While the Spanish got their ships ready, Francis Drake attacked the port of Cadiz and "singed the King of Spain's beard" by destroying 33 Spanish ships. The invasion was delayed for a year. But finally, in

Left: The Spanish Armada contained about twenty powerful galleons. They were slow and clumsy, and easy prey for the faster English ships.

1588, a fleet of about 130 ships set sail for England. It was called the *Armada*, which means "armed force" in Spanish.

Fighting the Enemy

As the huge fleet of ships came near the English coast, great beacons were lit from hilltop to hilltop, sending the message that the Armada was sighted. At first the Armada seemed impossible to conquer. It sailed up the English Channel. In August it anchored off the channel port of Calais, in France. The Spaniards were hoping to meet up with more Spanish troops from the Netherlands. While the Spanish were at anchor, the English navy attacked. The English ships were smaller and faster than the heavy Spanish galleons. During the night the English sent fire ships into the Armada. These were filled with gunpowder and set on fire. The Spanish ships were forced out to sea to escape the flames.

The English Victory

The English fleet chased the Armada, which quickly scattered in confusion. The Spanish were

Francis Drake began raiding Spanish colonies in South America in 1572 and helped to defeat the Armada in 1588. He was also the first Englishman to make a voyage around the world. On his return Queen Elizabeth knighted him on the deck of his ship *The Golden Hind*.

driven away to the north. It was the end of the proud Armada. Its ships made for home by sailing round the northern tip of Scotland and Ireland. Many were wrecked in storms along the treacherous coasts. Only about 60 battered Spanish ships reached home.

After the Armada, the Spanish navy gradually grew weaker. By the 1700s, the British navy ruled the seas.

A painting of the defeat of the Spanish Armada. In the front of the picture you can see a *galleass*, a cross between a galleon and a galley, rowed by many oarsmen. The English ships were faster and their guns could fire farther than those of the Spanish. They were able to fire again and again into the Spanish fleet while keeping out of range of the Spanish guns.

The Great Days of Sail

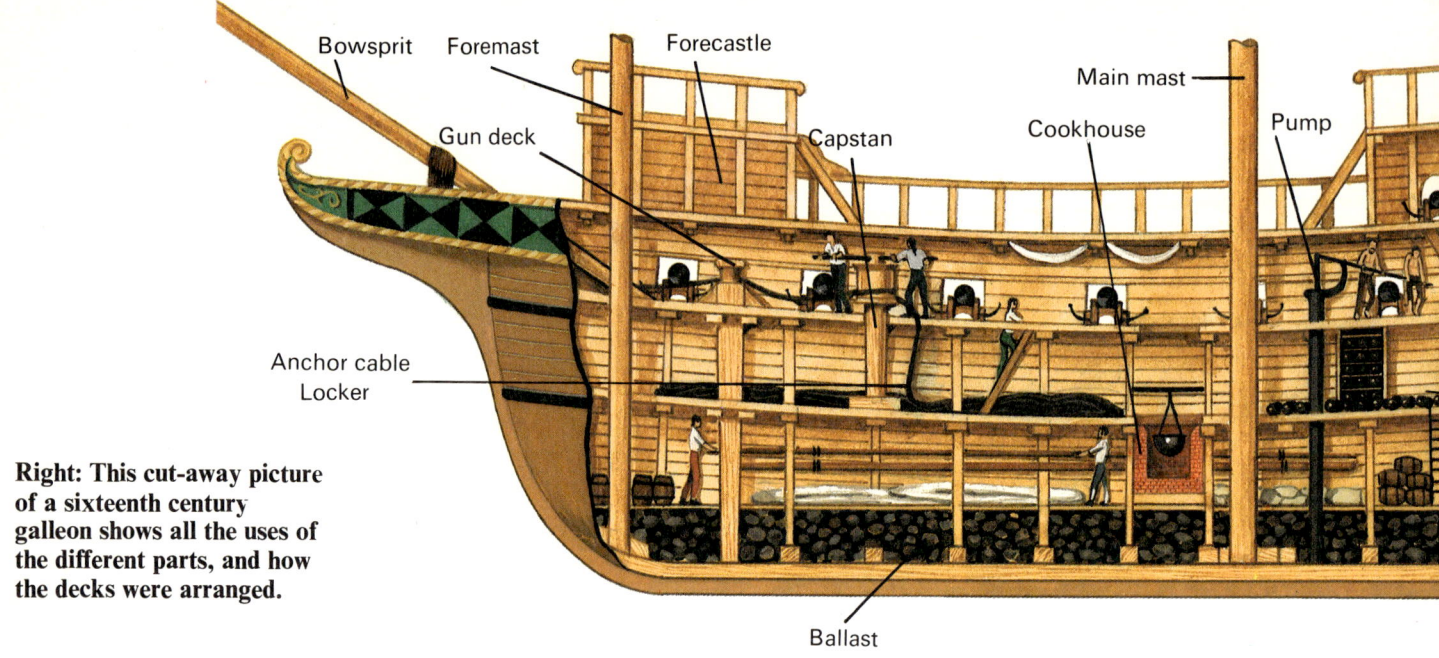

Bowsprit Foremast Forecastle Main mast Pump

Gun deck Capstan Cookhouse

Anchor cable
Locker

Ballast

Right: This cut-away picture of a sixteenth century galleon shows all the uses of the different parts, and how the decks were arranged.

The explorers who set out from Europe to sail across the unknown seas needed good ships in which to travel. By modern-day standards, the ships they used were tiny and dangerous. Many of them sank in storms around the world, and others were badly damaged. The ships' crews were often terrified by their journeys, and made ill by long months at sea without fresh food or water. Today we can only admire the ships that were built, and the men who sailed them, under such extraordinary conditions.

Below: The *Victory*, Admiral Nelson's flagship at the battle of Trafalgar in 1805. She was very little different from the galleons of the Spanish Armada.

Life on Board

The men who sailed on the early ships did not lead easy or comfortable lives. The ships were carefully built, but they were designed to make them sail fast and safely, not to be pleasant for the crew. Only the captain had a cabin to himself, and perhaps a bunk bed. The rest of the crew slept in hammocks, which were slung between posts anywhere in the body of the ship. The sailors were overcrowded and cramped in very small amounts of space.

The food on board ship was often terrible. Enough food was taken on before the ship sailed to last until they found land and fresh supplies. But if the journey took longer than expected, nothing could be done, and everyone had to make do with dry biscuits and stale water. Fresh food quickly went bad, so that was always eaten first. Without enough vitamins in their diet, the crew often got sick, and sometimes died.

As well as all the physical difficulties, the sailing ships' crews were often very frightened. No one knew what lands they would find when they set out, but there were lots of stories to worry them. Some people thought the Earth was flat, and that the ships would fall off the edge into empty space. Others thought they would be eaten by sea monsters. Stories like that sound a bit silly to us, but in those days it was easy to believe they were true.

Mizzen mast   Poop

Quarterdeck

Captain's cabin

Tiller

Cannonball store

Hold

Rudder

Right: This galleon setting sail shows what the outside of the cut-away picture looks like. The crew are unfurling the main sail.

Below: Ships like the *Cutty Sark* came much later than the galleons. She was a very fast clipper ship, used to bring tea from India and wool from Australia. Now the *Cutty Sark* has been restored, and can be seen in dry dock at Greenwich in London.

43

Christopher Columbus

Christopher Columbus was born in the Italian city of Genoa. He first went to sea when he was only 14, and sailed on trading ships around the Mediterranean. Later he sailed to the coast of Africa, but his great ambition was to discover a trade route to the rich eastern land of China. He thought he could do that by sailing west from Europe, across unknown seas.

Columbus tried to persuade the king of Portugal to send him, but the king refused. So Columbus tried the rulers of Spain, King Ferdinand and Queen Isabella. They listened to his arguments with interest, and in the end they agreed. Queen Isabella bought him three ships for his voyage, and helped him to find sailors for them. The ships were made ready with stores and equipment. Then, on 3 August 1492, Columbus set sail. The ships were called the *Santa Maria*, the *Nina* and the *Pinta*. Many people thought Columbus was mad to sail in uncharted waters with just three ships. Many of his crew thought the same, and were frightened that they might never return home.

Above: The three ships set sail from Spain for a new world.

44

The Journey

The ships faced many problems in their long journey. Mouldy food, stale water and cramped conditions made the sailors even more anxious about the idea, and the ships were old and slow – the *Pinta* soon needed repairs. But land was sighted in just over two months of sailing, and the relieved crews landed soon afterwards.

Columbus thought he had discovered an island to the east of Japan. He called the land San Salvador, and called the people he met there Indians. But, in fact, Columbus' ships had found a group of islands off the coast of North America. His ships sailed around the area for some time, charting the new lands, but Columbus never discovered his mistake.

On the journey home the *Santa Maria* was wrecked, and the other two ships were badly damaged. But eventually the rest of the crew and Columbus himself returned to Spain. Columbus was triumphant with his success, and believed great wealth would follow.

Above: This drawing is a reconstruction of the *Santa Maria*, in which Columbus sailed until it was shipwrecked on the journey home. This was the largest of the three ships, and carried a crew of about 40 men. Even so, by our standards, the *Santa Maria* was tiny: only 35.5 metres long.

Below: Columbus talks to Queen Isabella and King Ferdinand of Spain, to persude them to support his great venture across the Atlantic Ocean.

The Industrial Revolution

Two hundred and fifty years ago, there were no factories in Britain. Cloth was made by people in their own homes, and machines were not used for anything. The changes that happened during the next six hundred years altered everyone's lives for ever. These changes are called the Industrial Revolution, when a country that lived by farming became one filled with industry, machines and factories instead.

Machines to Make Cloth

The revolution began with cloth. Machines were invented that could be used to spin the yarn and weave the cloth much faster than it could be done by hand. A factory filled with machines like that could produce miles of material in a day. Then other machines were invented to do yet more jobs. Lots more factories were built around the coalfields, from where the fuel for the machines was brought. The factory owners became rich and powerful men.

Moving House

The factories employed lots of people, who had to move close to their new work. Many of them were poor and only used to country life. The factories were dangerous and filthy places, for there were no laws to say they should be safe and clean. Children as well as adults had to work for 12 hours a day, or even more. They earned almost no money for their work, and many were injured by the machines, or even killed.

Left: This old picture shows women working in a cloth factory, where steam engines were used to turn the machines. The machines were very dangerous to work with, and the hours were long and hard. The children in the picture had to work too.

Feeding the Cities

Everyone who lived in the new cities needed to have food grown for them, for they had no gardens of their own. This meant that farms changed as well – they grew bigger and more efficient. But the small farmers suffered too, for they could not afford new farming methods and lost some of their land to the sheep farmers. The picture above shows the difference between the smoky, dirty city and a rich landowner's estate.

The factory workers' homes were no better than the factories. They were small and crowded together, and many workers became ill from disease or from not eating enough.

It was many years before conditions got better for these people. But in the end, after years of misery, laws were passed to help them lead better lives and work in less dreadful conditions. But the houses stayed as they were – and some are still lived in today.

Right: An ironworks factory in the north of England. Here coke was first used to smelt iron to make bridges, ships and machines. Factories like this changed the countryside around them for ever, and changed the lives of everyone who worked there.

Early Railways

A man called George Stephenson was the founder of the railways. The engine below was built by him, and the railway on the right was begun by him. As the railways all over the world expanded from his ideas, he was in great demand everywhere to help develop them.

Stephenson had begun by building locomotives to be used in mines. Others had tried to build steam engines to carry people above ground, but they had failed. Today, steam engines are not used as much as electric or diesel ones – but without Stephenson's work, they might not exist at all.

Railways Take Off

Stephenson's first railway was the Stockton and Darlington, built in 1825. You can see a picture of it above. It was successful, and Stephenson soon built another one, the Liverpool and Manchester line, in 1830. The government approved of the new scheme, and soon 500 railway lines were built in Britain. Another great railway builder joined in too; a man called Isambard Kingdom Brunel, who was a famous engineer.

By 1870, only 45 years after the first railway was opened, there was almost 22,500 kilometres of railway track in Britain. Other countries, like the USA, followed suit.

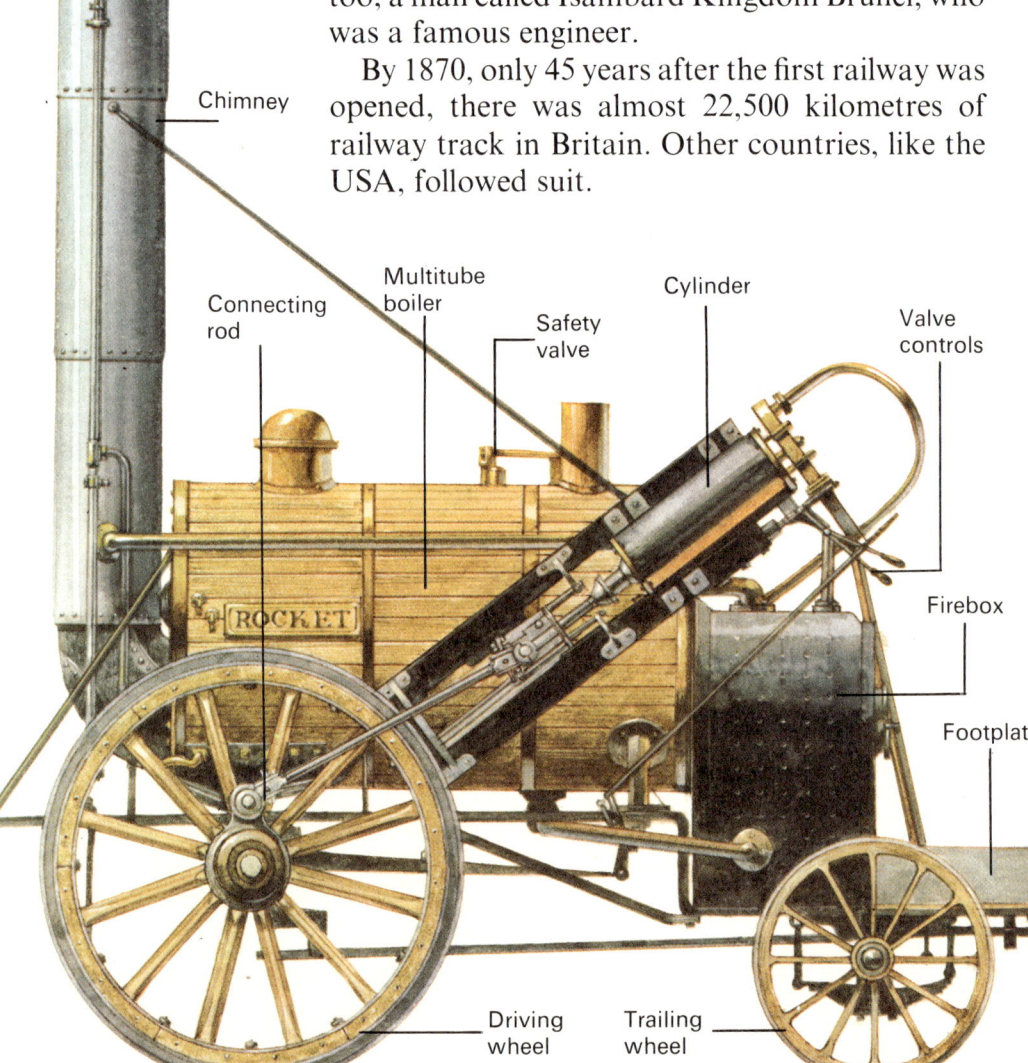

Right: Stephenson's engine, the Rocket, had a multitube boiler. This meant that heat was carried by lots of small tubes, and so steam could be raised more quickly with less fuel than other systems. It was a fast engine, but more important was the fact that it was strong and sturdy. It could haul heavy loads day after day and month after month. Earlier engines had not been able to take the strain of constant work.

Chimney

Connecting rod

Multitube boiler

Safety valve

Cylinder

Valve controls

Firebox

Footplate

ROCKET

Driving wheel

Trailing wheel

Train of Waggons drawn by a Loco-motive Engine.

Above: This picture was drawn by an artist when Stephenson's first railway opened. Three hundred people bought tickets for the first ride, but about twice that number managed to squeeze aboard!

Right: A typical locomotive in the USA in 1860. Its huge chimney was built to prevent sparks flying, and the "cow-catcher" on front cleared animals and any other obstructions off the track.

Water barrel

Tender

Laminated springs

American Railways

The first railway in the USA was opened in 1825. It was drawn by horses instead of an engine. But the British success with steam engines encouraged American companies to use them, and soon there were steam engines on public railways, pulling both freight cars and passenger carriages.

At first the railways faced a serious problem. Many of the tracks were built to different widths, called *gauges*. The same engine and carriages could not travel on tracks of different widths. But the railways were very important in the USA. They opened up parts of the country which had been too far away to reach easily any other way. Soon the gauge problems were solved, and by 1860 there were 50,000 kilometres of track.

The World of NATURE

Dinosaurs

Left: *Stegosaurus*, the largest of the plated dinosaurs, was 9 metres long. It had two rows of huge bony plates down its back, and horny spikes on its tail. Inside its head was a brain no bigger than a walnut.

Right: *Archaeopteryx*, the first bird, lived at the same time as the dinosaurs. It was about the size of a crow, and had clawed "fingers" on its wings. It could not fly, but probably clawed its way up trees and then glided down.

Stegosaurus

Archaeopteryx

Two hundred million years ago, huge, reptile-like monsters ruled the Earth. Today, we call these creatures dinosaurs, from Greek words that mean "terrible lizard". Some dinosaurs were as large as several houses. Other dinosaurs were no bigger than a chicken.

Plant-eaters

Some of the biggest animals ever to live on Earth were the plant-eating dinosaurs. One of these giants was *Apatosaurus*, once known as *Brontosaurus*, or "thunder lizard". Its legs were as thick as tree trunks, and it was 25 metres long from its tiny head to the tip of its long tail. Other plant-eaters included *Iguanodon*, which walked upright and had "hands" with spiky thumbs, and the duck-billed dinosaurs, called *hadrosaurs*. The armoured dinosaurs, such as *Triceratops* and *Stegosaurus*, were also plant-eaters. Some had huge, bony plates to protect them; others sprouted horns.

Terrible Teeth

King of the meat-eating dinosaurs was *Tyrannosaurus*. At 14 metres long, it was tall enough to peer into the upstairs window of a house. It had claws as long as carving knives on its front feet. Inside its jaws were rows of huge teeth, some as long as a man's hand. Other meat-eaters were small compared to *Tyrannosaurus*, but just as ferocious.

Scientists studying the fossil bones of these animals have been able to tell us a great deal about how they lived. Some think the dinosaurs were warm-blooded, like mammals. But we still do not know everything about them. One of the biggest unsolved mysteries is why, 65 million years ago, the dinosaurs suddenly died out. Many scientists think that the climate on Earth may have grown too cold for them.

Archaeopteryx

Tyrannosaurus

Stegosaurus

All About Shells

Right: Shells are made up of several different layers. The outside layer is horny and coloured.

Left: The outer layer may wear off. The thicker inner layers are made of a chalky material.

Mantle

Right: The shell is made by the mantle.

Horny Layer
Chalk layer
Mantle
Pearly layer

Left: The chalky middle layer is usually the thickest. The pearly layer can be thin.

The seashells we find on the beach are all the skeletons of a group of animals called molluscs. Most molluscs have their skeletons on the outside of their bodies. The skeletons, or shells, protect their soft bodies from other animals and from the waves. Molluscs include snails, mussels, clams and oysters. They also include the octopus, squid and cuttlefish, though these animals do not have shells.

The biggest group of molluscs are called *gastropods*. Most of these have a single shell that is coiled, as in winkles and whelks, or dome-shaped, as in limpets. The next biggest group of molluscs are called *bivalves*, because their shells are in two parts. Mussels, clams and oysters are all bivalves.

How Shells are Made
Molluscs grow shells rather as we grow nails. The shell is produced by a fold of skin called the *mantle*. It is built up

SHELLS ON SANDY BEACHES

Tiger Scallop
(3 cm wide)
It is not a beach shell but may be washed up.

Necklace Shell
(3 cm high)

Common Whelk
(8 cm high)

Common Cockle
(5.5 cm wide)
Burrows in sand from lower shore down and feeds at the surface.

Thin Tellin
feeding.

Prickly Cockle
(6 cm wide)

Thin Tellin
(2 cm long)

Blunt Tellin
(5.5 cm long)

Common Otter Shell
(15 cm long)

The beautiful pearly Nautilus (20 cm wide) swims in tropical waters. It is related to octopuses, squids and cuttlefishes. Of these, only the Nautilus has an outer shell.

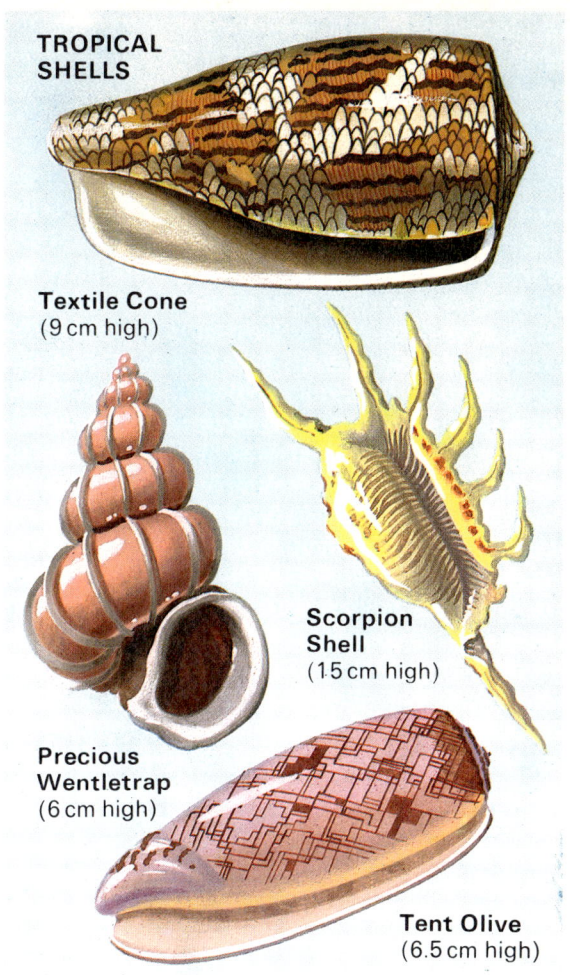

TROPICAL SHELLS

Textile Cone
(9 cm high)

Scorpion Shell
(15 cm high)

Precious Wentletrap
(6 cm high)

Tent Olive
(6.5 cm high)

in layers which harden and are dead, just as the ends of our nails are dead. Shell is made of a mixture of horn and chalky crystals which remains after the mollusc dies. The mollusc is attached to its shell by muscles. The shell grows with the animal.

Sandy and Rocky Shores

Most of the molluscs on sandy beaches are bivalves. It is difficult to find them because they bury themselves in the sand at low tide, away from the heat of the sun. But you may be able to dig up cockles or tellins carefully with a spade. On rocky beaches the molluscs are easier to find, as they cling to the surface of the rocks. Many are gastropods such as limpets, whelks and periwinkles. But mussels, which are bivalves, are common on rocky shores, too.

Using Shells

Since ancient times people have used shells for decoration. Some shells have been used as money. Others have been valuable for the dye they produce. Pearls, too, come from shells. The best pearls come from the pearl oyster. A pearl is made when a tiny piece of sand or grit irritates the mollusc's mantle. The animal covers it with shell lining to protect itself, and this turns into a pearl.

Magnifying glass

Tape measure

Spade

Tablespoon

Shrimping net

Plastic boxes

Plastic bags

Bucket

Sieve

Here are some of the things you will find useful for studying and collecting shells. It is sensible to wear old gym shoes, especially on a rocky beach.

The Great Apes

There are four kinds of apes, the animals most closely related to man: the chimpanzee, the orangutan, the gorilla and the gibbon. The biggest of these is the gorilla. This very strong animal has a huge chest, long arms and short legs. Standing up on its stout legs, the gorilla may be 2 metres tall. It can weigh more than 200 kilograms. The females are smaller.

The Gorillas at Home

Gorillas live in the rain forests of central Africa. They travel in groups of from 2 to 30, and one large male is always the leader of the group. In the picture the gorillas have spent the afternoon wandering among the tree creepers. They have been munching on wild celery, juicy leaves and roots. Now the sun is going down and the moist air is cooling. It is time for bed.

Every night the gorillas make big, untidy nests. The leader makes his first. He pulls branches and leaves into a rough circle around him. Then he pushes softer leaves and twigs underneath him, to make a mattress. When he is comfortable, the others start to build their nests. The older males make their nests on the ground. They are too heavy to sleep in the trees. The younger gorillas are lighter and can climb more easily. They make their beds in the safety of the trees.

Baby Gorillas

The mother gorilla makes a nest big enough for herself and her baby. She tears down leafy branches and twigs, weaving them together. Often she makes her nest in a tree.

A baby gorilla weighs about 2 kilograms when it is born. At first the mother carries the baby about in her arms. After about three months the baby is strong enough to hold on to its mother by itself. It can walk by about 5 months.

The Fastest Animals

The fastest animals on land, in water, and in the air are all hunters. They use speed to catch their prey. Other animals use speed for the opposite reason – to escape being caught.

Fastest of All

The fastest of all animals is a bird, the spine-tailed swift. It can fly at up to 170 km an hour while chasing insects. Spine-tailed swifts spend most of their time in the air. They live on rock ledges and "take off" by diving into the air.

Other fast-flying birds include golden eagles and peregrine falcons. They can reach speeds of more than 100 km an hour when diving after their prey. At sea, frigate birds may be blown along in a gale at even higher speeds.

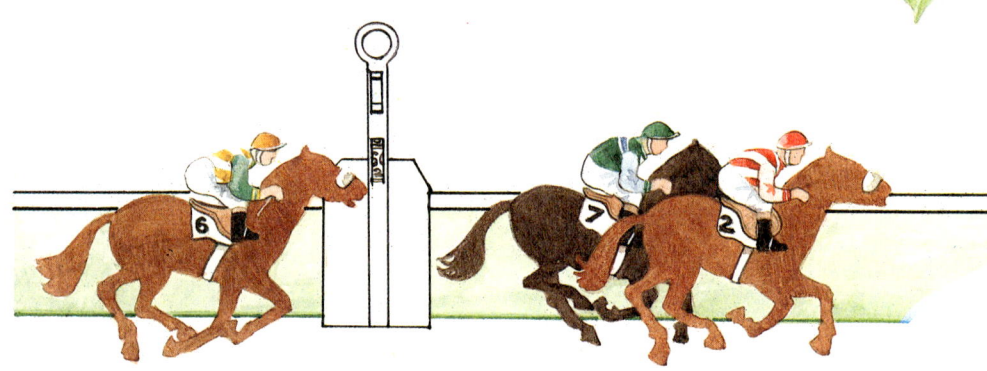

Above: A high-seed camera can also freeze the rapid wing-beat of a hovering hummingbird. Hummingbirds' wings appear to "whirr" as they hover. They may beat their wings more than 60 times in just one second.

Above: Many things happen too quickly for our eyes to see. But a high-speed camera can "freeze" these moments for us. Without high-speed photography, judges could not tell the winners of close horse races. The camera photographs the horses as they speed past the winning post. A finish decided by camera is called a "photo-finish".

Right: A cheetah runs in hot pursuit of its prey. Though it is one of the big cats, the cheetah is built more like a dog. Its body is slim like that of a greyhound. A deep chest allows it to breathe in plenty of oxygen to fuel its high speeds. It has a small head and long, slender legs. A cheetah must bring down its prey quickly for it cannot keep up its top speeds for long.

Mammal Record-breakers

The cheetah is the fastest mammal. It can run at speeds up to about 100 km an hour, but only in short bursts. If the cheetah does not catch its prey quickly, the prey can usually outrun it. Antelopes and gazelles are better long-distance runners. The pronghorn antelope can keep going at a steady 56 km an hour for many minutes.

Fast and Slow Animals

A racehorse carrying a rider can run at 70 km an hour, and the best greyhounds have been timed at about 60 km an hour. The fastest fish is the sailfish, which can speed through the water at more than 60 km an hour. Elsewhere in the animal world, speeds are not so fast. Snakes often appear to move quickly, but the fastest speed measured is only 11 km an hour, for the black mamba of Africa.

No one gets prizes for being slowest, but if they did, the sea anemone might win. It crawls over rocks under the sea at only 6 mm a minute – so slowly that many people do not realize it can move at all. Compared with sea anemones, common garden snails seem like racehorses – they cover an amazing 15 cm in one minute!

Right: The sailfish, the fastest creature in the sea, has a strong, torpedo-shaped body. When it is moving at speed, the sailfish folds its sail-like fin down into a groove in its back. This makes it even more streamlined.

Left: The spine-tailed swift is the fastest creature in the world.

Animal Homes

Our Earth is the home of many different kinds of animals with many different ways of life. On these pages you can see just a few of the strange homes used by creatures that share our planet.

The elf owl lives in the desert. Its home is a hole in a giant cactus. The ovenbird of South America builds a clay nest shaped like an old-fashioned baker's oven. The water spider spins a little silken bag under water. It fills the bag with air bubbles which it brings to the surface. This diving bell is its home. The mouth breeder is one of several kinds of fish that carry their eggs and their young around in their mouths.

Ovenbird

Elf owl

Water spider

Mouth breeder

Fox

Rabbit

A great many animals make their homes underground. Few enemies can get in, and the homes are warm and cosy.

A badger's home is called a set. Each set has several entrances and many passages and rooms. The tidy badgers keep their set clean by taking all the rubbish out.

The home of a fox is called an earth. The fox likes to borrow its home rather than dig it for itself.

Rabbits dig burrows that are a maze of rambling tunnels. The bumblebee builds wax cells for her eggs in a small hole – perhaps an old mouse hole.

Moles spend most of the time underground. They dig tunnels with their strong front feet, pushing the soil away with their back feet. Slugs hide underground during the day so that the sun does not dry them up. Earthworms burrow by swallowing the soil and passing it out behind them.

Badger

Mole

Slug

Earthworm

Bumblebee

Birds

Crown

Neck

Nape

Back

Rump

Tail

Beak or bill

Chin

Throat

Breast

Belly

Feet

Primary feathers

Secondary feathers

Flank

Legs

Above: This picture shows the parts of a bird's body. The bird is a male redstart.

Most birds have a very poor sense of smell, and rely most on their sight. Some birds, such as hawks, have eyes which are ten times as good as human eyes. Hunting birds' eyes are placed at the front of their heads so they can watch their prey easily. Smaller birds' eyes are placed at the sides of their heads. They can look for food and watch for enemies at the same time.

Beaks for all diets
Birds' beaks vary a lot, depending on what they eat. 1 House sparrow (cracking seeds) 2 Swallow (wide space for flying insects) 3 Kingfisher (fish) 4 Duck (straining food from the water) 5 Crow (all-purpose) 6 Woodpecker (sharp for probing bark) 7 Sparrowhawk (flesh) 8 Curlew (sharp for probing mud) 9 Wren (insects).

Although birds do not have ears like humans have, with a special flap to help sound waves reach the brain, they do have very good hearing. But many birds, although they can hear the smallest sounds, cannot always tell from which direction the sound comes.

Gliding and Flying

The very first birds could not fly at all, and probably used their wings to help them glide through the air. Some birds today still use their wings to glide rather than to fly, but birds' wings are specially developed for flight.

A bird's wing feathers open and close as the bird moves its wings to fly. When the wings press down the feathers are tightly closed, and push against the air underneath. When the wings press up the feathers open again, to let the air through. This means the bird does not have to work so hard to push against the air.

Staying Aloft

Birds which do not flap, or beat, their wings in flight use breezes and air currents to stay aloft. Gliding birds generally have very long wings, which help them to catch as much of the air movement as possible. A bird such as the albatross can glide for very long distances without flapping its wings at all. Kestrels and vultures use air currents to stay aloft for hours. They watch the ground for prey, and dive suddenly when they see something to eat.

Migration

A lot of birds fly from one part of the Earth to another, and later return to where they came from. They leave a place where food is getting hard to find and go to another where food is plentiful. This is called *migration*, and birds may fly more than 15,000 kilometres every year.

Swallows live in Africa, but when winter comes to that country the swallows fly north to Europe, where the summer is just beginning. There they lay their eggs, hatch their young and rear them. At the end of the northern summer the swallows return to Africa with their young which have learned to fly. In Africa, the summer is just beginning when they return. Swallows must migrate because they feed on flying insects, and these are very scarce in the winter time.

Birds migrate in large flocks, to help protect themselves from their enemies. Some fly in formation as well. They all use the sun as a guide.

Magpie

Crow

Rook

Above: You can often see these three birds in both towns and in the countryside. Rooks and crows are generally seen in groups, but magpies are common alone, or in pairs.

Below: These birds are common in Britain: the ones on the left can often be seen in towns, but those on the right mostly stay in the country, and in woodland.

TOWN BIRDS	WOODLAND BIRDS

Mistle thrush

Blackbird

Long-tailed tit

Blue tit

Dunnock

Greenfinch

Wren

Robin

Green woodpecker

Woodpigeon

Sparrow-hawk

Bullfinch

Blackcap

Treecreeper

Chiffchaff

Great tit

Insects

There are more insects than any other kind of animal on Earth. In fact, there are probably about one million different kinds of insects. Only a few live in the sea, but you can find insects everywhere else. Some, such as butterflies and moths, are beautiful to look at. Others, such as ants and bees, amaze us with their complicated colonies, in which each insect has a special job to do. Still others eat our crops or carry dangerous diseases.

What is an Insect?

Insects are many shapes and sizes, but it is easy to recognize one. Its body is divided into three parts: the head, the thorax and the abdomen. On the head are two antennae, or feelers. On the thorax are three pairs of legs. Most adult insects also have wings. The shape of the wings helps us to identify the insect. Flies have only two wings, but most other insects have four.

Many young insects look very different from the adults. They go through several different stages as they grow up. The change that takes place is called *metamorphosis*.

Below: A ladybird folds its hind wings under its tough front wings after flying. A ladybird is a beetle. Beetles have biting jaws and their hard front wings meet in a straight line down the centre of their body.

Ladybird

Right: The head of a beetle, showing its strong biting jaws.

Rose chafer

Below left: A ladybird eats greenfly.

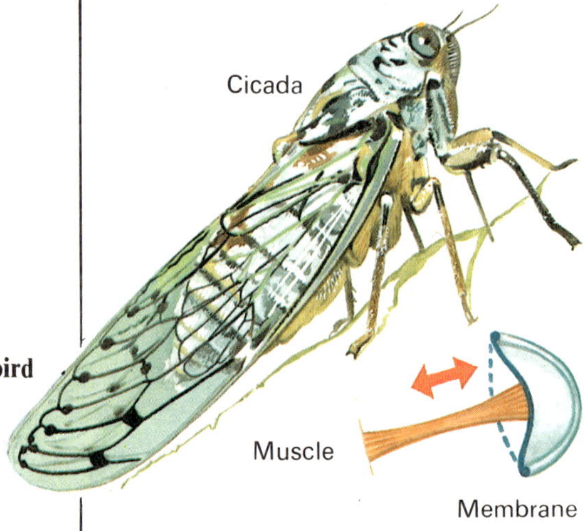

Greenfly

Leaf beetles

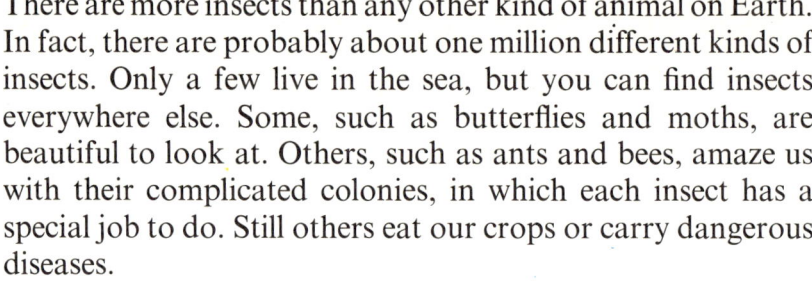

Cicada

Muscle

Membrane

Cicadas are insects that suck the juices, or sap, from plants. The males are very noisy. A membrane on each side of the body vibrates at high speed like a miniature drum-skin. This produces a shrill, whistle-like sound which attracts the females.

Below: Burying beetles bury dead animals and lay eggs on them.

Burying

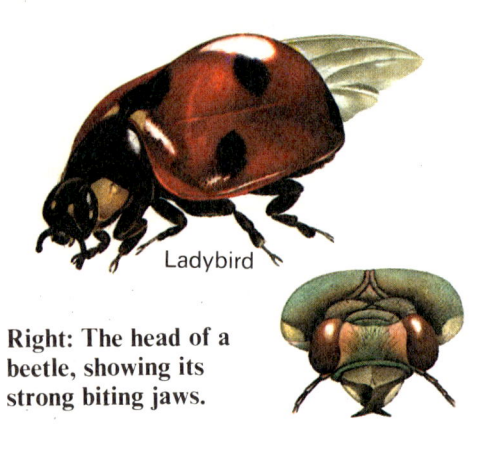

BUTTERFLIES OF THE FIELDS

Wall brown

Meadow brown

Small heath

Marbled white

Swallowtail

Grizzled skipper

Small copper

Clouded yellow

Chalkhill blue

Common blue

Heath fritillary

Dark green fritillary

All these butterflies live in the fields of Britain and Europe. Butterflies are among the most beautiful insects. If you have a garden, you can attract many kinds of butterfly by planting flowers that are rich in nectar for them to feed on. You can watch them plunging their long tongues into the flowers to suck up the nectar. When they are not feeding, their tongues are coiled up.

The patterns on a butterfly's wings are made from thousands of tiny scales too small to see without the help of a microscope.

The Life of an Insect

The life of a butterfly shows us how metamorphosis works. The female butterfly lays her eggs on a leaf. The eggs hatch into tiny *larvae*, called caterpillars. Each caterpillar feeds on leaves and grows steadily. When it is ready, it spins a silken cocoon around itself with a special, thread-like material from its body. The caterpillar enters the resting stage known as the *pupa* or *chrysalis*. Here metamorphosis takes place. The adult butterfly eats its way out of the cocoon, spreads its wings and flies away. Soon it will lay its own eggs, and the cycle will begin again.

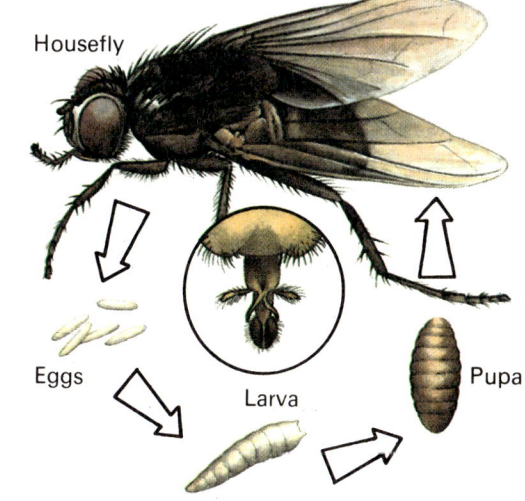

Housefly

Eggs

Larva

Pupa

Right: The life cycle of a housefly may take only a week. A close-up of the fly's sponge-like mouth is shown in the circle.

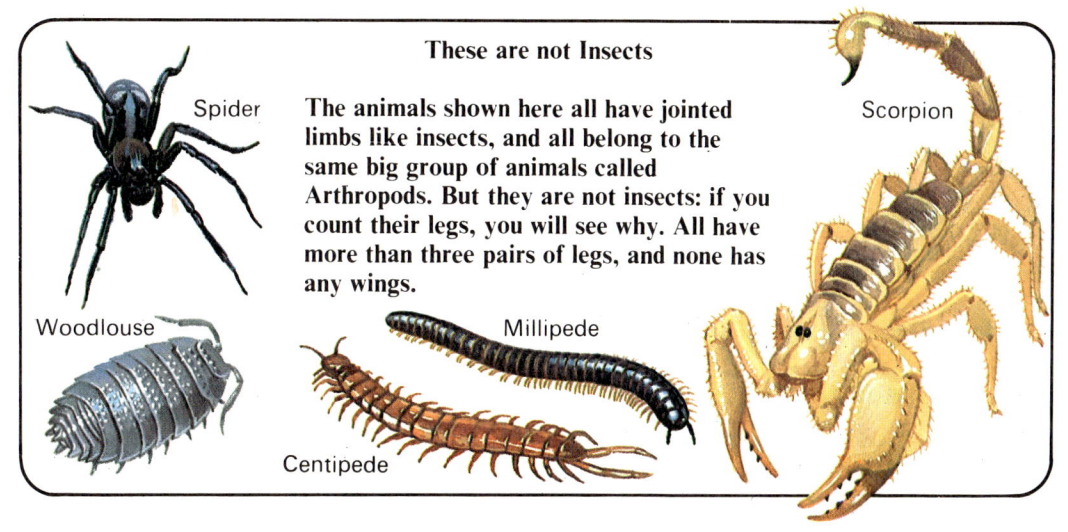

These are not Insects

Spider

Scorpion

The animals shown here all have jointed limbs like insects, and all belong to the same big group of animals called Arthropods. But they are not insects: if you count their legs, you will see why. All have more than three pairs of legs, and none has any wings.

Woodlouse

Millipede

Centipede

All About Dogs

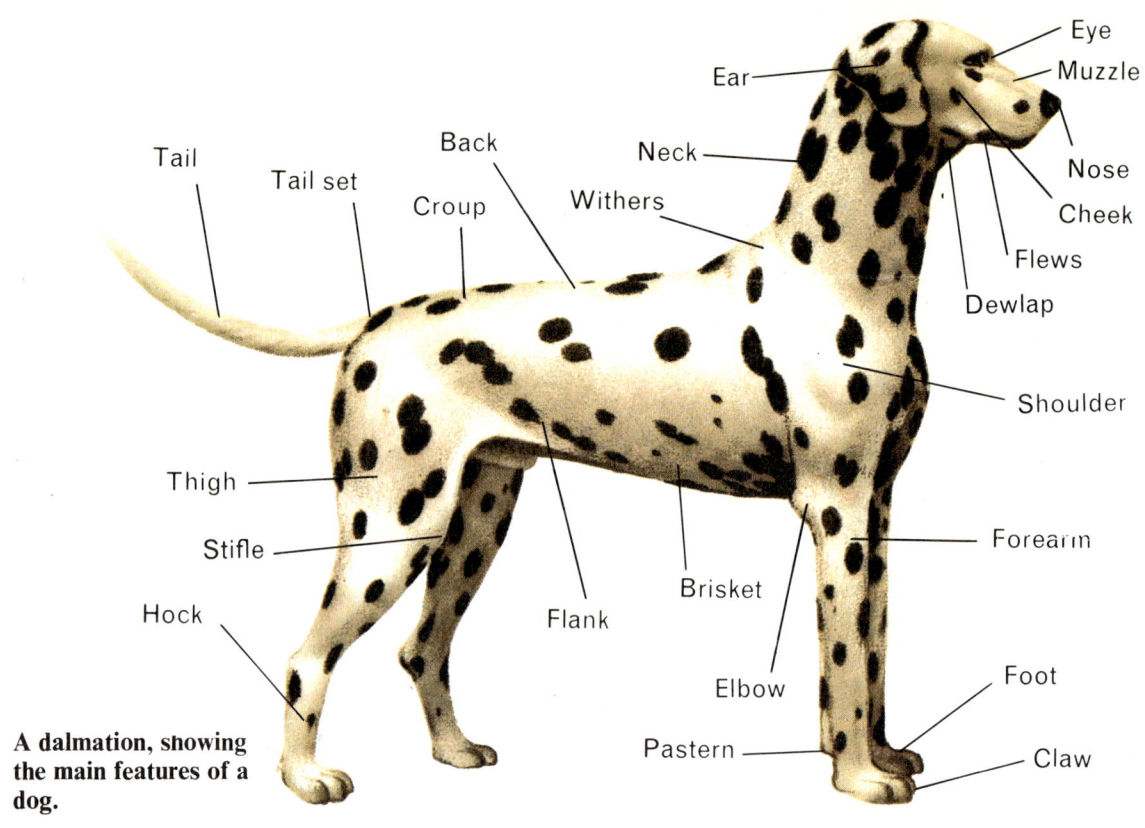

Tail
Tail set
Back
Croup
Withers
Neck
Ear
Eye
Muzzle
Nose
Cheek
Flews
Dewlap
Shoulder
Thigh
Stifle
Forearm
Hock
Flank
Brisket
Elbow
Pastern
Foot
Claw

A dalmation, showing the main features of a dog.

Dogs were the first animal to be tamed by man. The dog family includes not only the many breeds of tame dogs, but wild dogs as well. Wolves, foxes, jackals and hyenas are all related to the dogs we keep as pets.

Living in Packs

In the wild, dogs are "social" animals. They live in groups or packs. They hunt for their food, chasing other animals. Early man was a hunter, too. At first, the dog was a rival in the hunt for food. Later, people realized that the dog would be a useful helper. And so pups were trained to be hunting dogs.

The Dog's Family Tree
Dogs today are descended from a prehistoric animal called Cynodictus. The picture shows the dog's "family tree". The tame dog's closest relative in the wild is the wolf. There are different wild dogs in various parts of the world. Most of them, like the wolves and jackals, live in packs.

Your pet dog no longer lives in a pack with other dogs. Instead he shares your home. Your family is his "pack". He obeys its rules just as he would if he were living in the wild. Some dogs are still used for hunting. And all dogs still have some instinct to hunt.

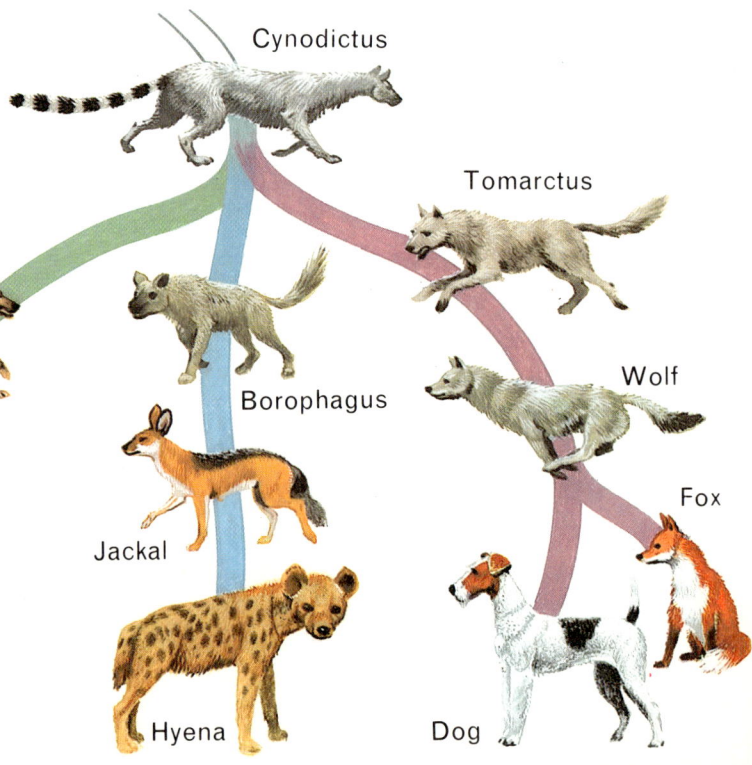

Cynodictus
Tomarctus
Lycaon
Borophagus
Wolf
Jackal
Fox
African Hunting Dog
Hyena
Dog

Training a Dog Dogs enjoy training. Teach one thing at a time. Be patient.

Sit Hold the collar, to keep dog's head up. Push its rear down.

Down Teach this once your dog has learned to sit. Slide its front paws out from under it.

Heel Teach your dog to walk beside you, without pulling.

Come Begin with the dog on the lead, to make it come to you.

Stay Train the dog to stay still until you tell it to "come".

Do's and Don'ts Do praise your dog. Don't lose your temper.

All Kinds of Dogs

Over hundreds of years many different breeds of dog have been developed. There are hunting dogs (hounds), gundogs (retrievers, spaniels and setters, for example), sheepdogs, guard dogs and other "working dogs". But today most dogs do not work. They are kept as pets or for show. "Toy" dogs have been popular pets for thousands of years.

Dogs come in all shapes and sizes. The tiny Chihuahau weighs less than a kilogram, whereas the huge St Bernard can weigh as much as 86 kilograms.

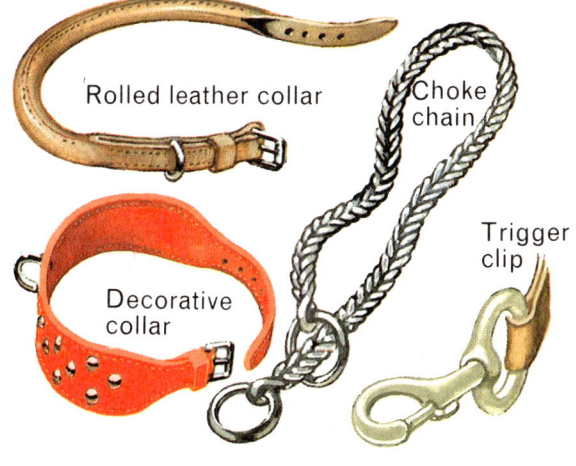

Rolled leather collar

Choke chain

Decorative collar

Trigger clip

Dogs can be trained to pull sledges and carts. Husky dogs are useful working animals in the Arctic. Sled teams like this can drag loads across the ice and snow.

Your dog should always wear a collar, with its name and address on. In town, a dog should be kept on the lead, especially when there are cars about. The choke chain is worn by strong dogs which keep pulling on the lead. The best lead clip is the trigger clip shown above.

67

Horses and Ponies

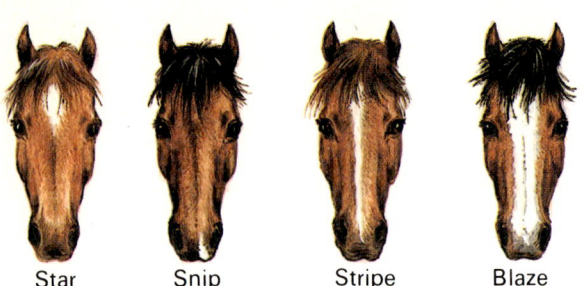

Horses sometimes have different shaped white marks on their faces. Here are four, with their names.

Star   Snip   Stripe   Blaze

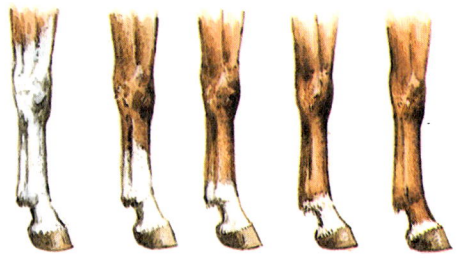

Stocking Sock Fetlock Pastern Coronet

A horse's feet and legs may also have distinctive markings. If the mark reaches above the knee it is called a stocking. A smaller mark is known as a sock, and so on, down to the coronet.

The First Horses

The ancestors of the horse lived millions of years ago. They were small, shy animals of the woodland. They ran quickly to escape their enemies. Later horse-like animals lived on the open grassy plains. For greater speed, they ran on tip-toe. The modern horse has lost the use of all its toes, save one, which we call the hoof.

The horse was one of the first animals to be tamed by man. At first men hunted horses for food. But the horse was far more useful as a beast of burden, carrying riders and pulling wagons. Until the 1700s, and the coming of the steam engine, horse-power was man's most useful ally.

Horses Today

Today, only a few wild horses remain. The great Shires remind us of the heavy horses which once pulled ploughs and carts. The finest of all riding horses is the Thoroughbred. All modern Thoroughbreds are descended from three Arab horses which were cross-bred with English hunters in the 1800s. The smallest and most sure-footed of horses is the pony.

A male horse is called a stallion. The female is a mare, and the young are known as foals.

Points of the Horse
The different parts of a horse are known as its "points". This picture shows you where the main points are. The height of horses and ponies is measured in hands. One hand equals 10 cm. The largest Shire horses stand over 17 hands high. Most ponies are under 14 hands. The little Shetland pony is only about 9 hands high.

Ear, Forelock, Poll, Mane, Withers, Back, Flank, Loins, Croup, Dock, Tail, Eye, Thigh, Cheek, Muzzle, Shoulder, Chest, Forearm, Sheath, Belly, Hock, Knee, Chestnut, Fore cannon, Hind cannon, Pastern, Fetlock, Ergot, Hoof, Heel

Caring for a Pony

Ponies need proper food, water and plenty of exercise. They are happiest kept in a grassy field, with other ponies for company. The stable must be cleaned every day. The pony will need grooming every day too, with a good brush to keep its coat healthy. Iron horse shoes prevent the hooves from wearing down, and need to be replaced at regular intervals.

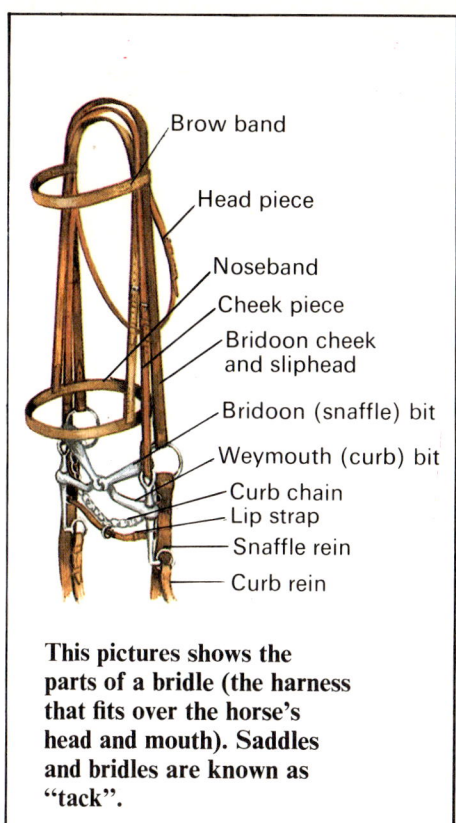

Brow band

Head piece

Noseband

Cheek piece

Bridoon cheek and sliphead

Bridoon (snaffle) bit

Weymouth (curb) bit

Curb chain

Lip strap

Snaffle rein

Curb rein

This pictures shows the parts of a bridle (the harness that fits over the horse's head and mouth). Saddles and bridles are known as "tack".

Shown below are ponies from several parts of the world. Ponies are tough, even-tempered animals. They make good working horses as well as pets.

Criollo: A cattle pony from South America

Basuto: A tough pony from South Africa

Falabella: This tiny Argentine pony is usually kept as a pet

Australian pony

Pony of the Americas

Hocaido: A fast Japanese pony

Cats of all Kinds

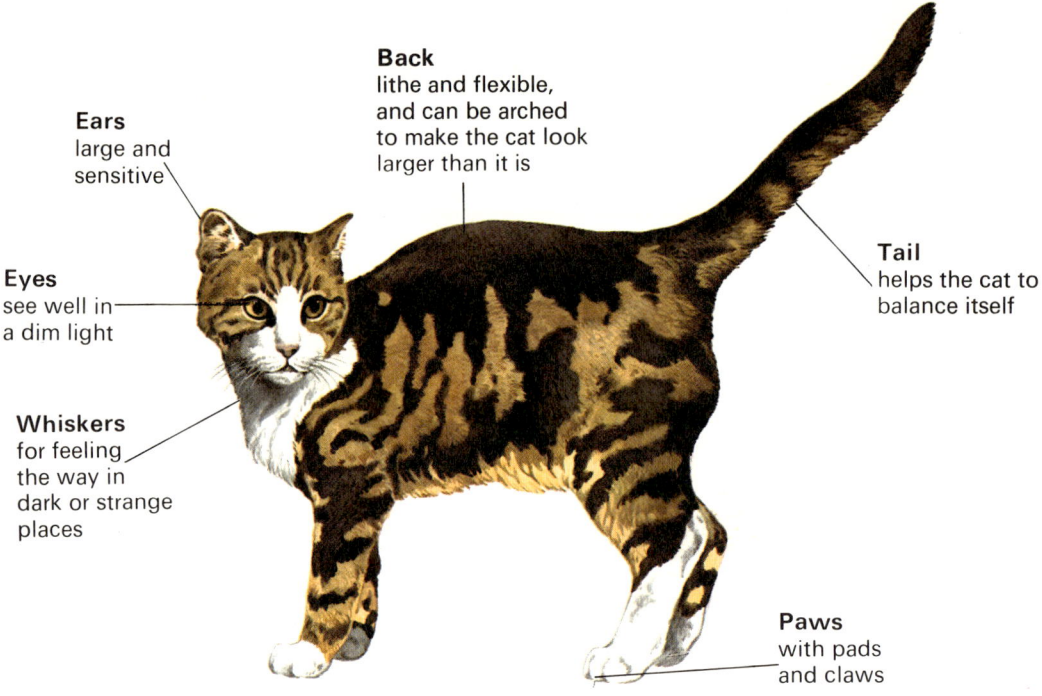

Ears large and sensitive

Back lithe and flexible, and can be arched to make the cat look larger than it is

Eyes see well in a dim light

Whiskers for feeling the way in dark or strange places

Tail helps the cat to balance itself

Paws with pads and claws

Our domestic cats are the smallest members of the cat family. A lion, which can grow as long as 3 metres from head to tail, is the biggest member of the same family of animals. You might not think that a pet cat and a wild lion have much in common, but there are lots of things they share.

Hunting for Food

A pet cat does not generally need to hunt its food, but even a young kitten will practise doing this. It will spend hours of its time stalking and pouncing on leaves, balls of wool, or anything else that seems suitable. The kitten learns to flatten its ears, to move silently and slowly, and to pounce only at the last possible moment. All these skills are used by its wild relatives like lions and tigers. The kitten is doing in play what once was needed just to stay alive.

Seeing in the Dark

Cats cannot see in complete darkness, but their eyes are very good at using whatever light there is at night. This, too, is a hunting skill. Being able to see in a dim light, added to the excellent hearing which all cats have, makes them a dangerous enemy.

The Colour of Cats

Pedigree cats are bred to a plan which means that their owners know what colour the kittens may be. The colour of a cat is fixed by the colour of its parents and some colours are bound to repeat themselves in the kittens. Tabby markings are very strong, and keep showing in kittens for many generations. Other colours are not so strong, and only appear in kittens if both parents have the colour themselves. Some colours are linked to the cat's sex. A ginger cat without any white fur is usually male, and a tortoiseshell cat is always female.

Some colours are thought to be lucky – like black cats. But there are lots to choose from!

Paws and Claws

Cats walk on their toes, and the soft pads on their paws help them to move silently when they are stalking their prey. Their claws are very sharp, and these can be *retracted* into hard sheaths between their pads when they are not in use. Cats use their claws for climbing steep or rough surfaces such as tree trunks, and also for holding down their prey. If you watch two cats playing, you will see them use their claws in many different ways. The back

Blue-eyed white

Odd-eyed white

Orange-eyed white

Longhaired white cats can have three different eye colours: blue, orange, or one eye of each colour. The cats with blue eyes are sometimes deaf.

claws are often used to slash at their opponents, while the front claws hit out.

Moving Around

All cats have long, sleek and agile bodies. Their muscles are specially arranged so that the cats can spring, jump and climb with ease. Most cats can balance very well on narrow ledges, and they seldom fall. Even then, their bodies are so flexible that they generally can twist around in the air and land safely on their paws. Cats' tails help them to balance, too. If you have a pet cat, you can learn how your cat is feeling by watching how it holds its tail. A fluffed-out tail is a sign of anger or fear.

A tortoiseshell and her kittens.

Tortoiseshell cats have coats with a mixture of ginger, cream and black. They are always female. Tortoiseshell cats, if they mate with a ginger or black tom, can have tortoiseshell kittens.

Self coloured

Standard tabby

Mackerel tabby

Tortoiseshell and white

Tortoiseshell

Spotted

Smoke

Bi-coloured

Colour-pointed

Animals with Pouches

Animals which have pouches in which to carry their young are called *marsupials*. The best-known marsupial is the Australian kangaroo. All marsupials live in Australia except the American opossum.

The Young Kangaroo

When a kangaroo is about to give birth, she first cleans out her pouch, then lies on her side. The new-born baby looks very little like a kangaroo. It is barely two centimetres long, with front legs slightly longer than its back legs. It is quite blind and has not yet grown ears. It takes about three minutes to crawl into its mother's pouch, where it clings to a teat and begins to suck milk from it. There it stays for six or seven months.

The growing baby rides everywhere in its mother's pouch until it is big enough to stand. At last, it starts to make longer and longer trips on foot. At the first sign of danger, however, it dives head first back into the pouch, turning a quick somersault inside to poke out its head again. After a while the mother has to turn it out, when it grows too big or when another new baby is growing in there.

The Koala Bear

The Australian koala bear is not a bear at all. It just looks like one. It is a marsupial, like the kangaroo. This mother's pouch opens backwards. The tiny, ill-formed baby takes six months to grow large enough to leave the pouch and ride on its mother's back. Koalas move slowly about among the branches of eucalyptus trees and hardly ever touch the ground. Their only food is leaves from the eucalyptus tree.

Forest fires and hunting nearly wiped out all the koalas, but now many live safely in reserves.

The Busy Beaver

Have you heard a person say that someone is as busy as a beaver? No wonder people say this about someone who is working hard. Beavers really do spend most of their lives hard at work.

Beavers are perhaps he cleverest home builders of all animals. The home is called a *lodge*, and it is built of logs, branches and mud. Whole families take part in building the house.

The beaver house is built in a pond or lake. First they build a platform of mud and twigs until it is above water level. On top of the platform they build a dome-shaped room which may be 3 metres across. The beavers get into the room by swimming into it through underwater tunnels. So the house is safe from enemies such as bears and wolves.

Building a Dam

If the beavers cannot find a pond or shallow lake, they make one by building a dam across a stream. To make the dam, the beavers cut down small trees with their strong, sharp front teeth. They chew off branches and drag them to the stream. There they bury the end of the branches in the mud. This is the foundation for their dam. Round the branches they pile more twigs, mud and sometimes stones until a strong barrier is built.

Beaver dams have been found that are 300

The beaver's front feet are like hands (left). They have five toes with long, thick claws. The front feet are used for picking things up and carrying.

In the picture below you can see inside the beaver's lodge and the underwater tunnels leading to it. A beaver is repairing the dam, while another cuts down a tree with its chisel-sharp front teeth.

The female beaver has a litter of two to five kits in the spring (above). They are out learning to swim when they are a month old. But they stay with their parents for two years.

metres long and over 2 metres high. They are strong enough for a horse to walk along the top.

What Beavers Eat

Beavers are big eaters. They feed on the bark and young shoots of trees. During the summer they gather a big store of branches under the water near their lodge. This is their winter food supply.

Where do Beavers Live?

Beavers live mainly in North America, although there are still a few in Europe. Hunters killed so many beavers for their fur that there were very few left. Laws were passed to protect the animals. Today they can only be hunted at certain times of the year. Their numbers are increasing.

A Useful Tail

The beaver's tail is broad and scaly. It is used as a rudder when swimming and as a support when it sits up to cut down trees. When the beaver wants to warn other beavers of some danger, it slaps its broad tail on the water to make a loud noise.

A Wonderful Swimmer

The beaver is very much at home under water. It can stay down for as much as 15 minutes because it has very big lungs for its size. The North American beaver is about a metre long, including its tail. It weighs about 25 kilograms.

The beaver's teeth keep on growing all through the animal's life. This makes up for the wearing-away of the busy animal's teeth by all the chewing that it does.

Trees

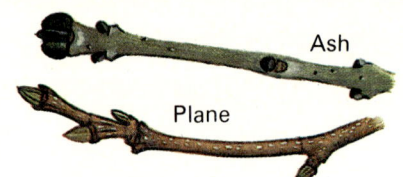

Winter buds hold the next season's leaves, and sometimes the flowers as well.

In spring watch horse chestnut buds burst open in a jar of water. See the sticky bud scales fold back to reveal the leaves. Time how long the leaves take to open. Notice which of the buds have flowers in them.

The trees below produce separate male and female flowers. Tassel-like catkins are groups of male flowers containing pollen. Wind or insects may carry pollen to the female flowers. Pollen may fertilize a female flower that it lands on. Fertilized flowers produce seeds that fall to the ground. Some seeds grow into young trees.

Trees include the largest, tallest and oldest living things on Earth. The largest is a California big tree. You could make 5000 million matches from its wood. The tallest is a coast redwood more than 111 metres high. The oldest tree is a bristlecone pine 4600 years old. All three grow in California.

Trees are plants with woody trunks that help them spread leafy branches high above the ground to reach the light. There are thousands of kinds of tree but only two main groups. These are the broad-leafed trees and the conifers.

Broad-leafed trees

These trees have broad, flat leaves. Most kinds are deciduous. This means they shed their leaves in a cold or dry part of the year.

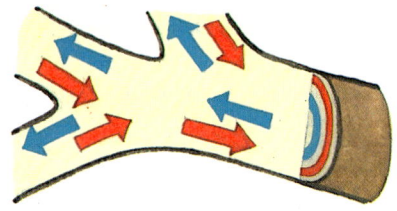

Branches contain many tiny tubes which carry water and minerals to the leaves, and food away from them.

Cherry   Pine

The dead and cracked outer bark protects the living trunk underneath.

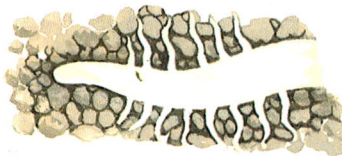

Roots anchor the tree in the ground. The root hairs take in water and minerals from the soil.

Lombardy poplar   Ash   Aspen   Elm   Common lime

Horse chestnut — Fruit, Seed
Common walnut — Fruit, Stone, Seed
Beech — Husk, Nut
Sweet chestnut — Husk, Nut

Broad-leafed trees include ash, elm, chestnut, maple, oak and holly. Many have hard wood useful for making tools or furniture. People usually call all of them hardwood trees, although the wood of broad-leafed trees like the silver birch is really very soft.

Conifers

Conifers are trees with leaves that look like green needles. They are called conifers because they bear their seeds in cones. Most conifers have leaves all the year round. Such trees are known as evergreens.

Conifers include the cypresses, larches, pines and spruces. Many have soft wood. Machines mash up huge quantities for making paper. People usually call all conifers softwood trees, yet some have very hard wood.

The pollinated flowers of many woodland trees produce seeds protected by fruits with tough, woody coats. These fruits are called nuts. Beech nuts and sweet chestnuts are common examples.

1. Douglas fir
2. Scot's pine
3. Monterey pine
4. Deodar
5. Common yew
6. Cypress

The needle-like leaves of conifers may be borne singly (1 and 5), in pairs (2), in threes (3), or in whorls (4). Cypresses (6) have scale-like leaves.

rnbeam   Crack willow   Silver birch

77

Wild Flowers

The picture shows a flower cut through the centre so that you can see the different parts. There are five petals and ten stamens in the complete flower.

Stigma
Style
Ovary
} Carpel

The carpel produces the fruit and seed

Stamen } Anther / Filament

The anthers produce the pollen

Petal: brightly coloured to attract insects

Stem: holds the leaves and flowers up to the light

Sepal: protects the flower when it is in bud

Leaf: where the plant makes most of its food

Ovule: seeds develop from the ovule

Bud: an unopened flower

Receptacle: the top of the flower stalk, to which all parts of the flower are attached

PARTS OF A FLOWER
Meadow cranesbill

Wild flowers grow almost anywhere – in towns as well as in the country. Many of them are very beautiful and are easy to recognize. Some, such as the dog violet, are small and delicate. Others, such as the foxglove, are large and colourful.

Where Flowers Grow

Some wild flowers like shady woodlands; others prefer sunny meadows. Still others grow along streams or on high mountain slopes. Beaches and seashores have plants that can stand large amounts of salt. Many seeds find their way into towns. They take root on waste ground and in railway yards, in pavement cracks, on old walls, and in town gardens.

Recognizing Wild Flowers

When the plants are not in flower, you can often recognize them by their leaves. Plants growing in shady places often

SOME WHITE WOODLAND FLOWERS

White helleborine (Summer)

Wood anemone (Spring)

Wild Strawberry (Spring and early summer)

Dog's mercury (Early spring)

Fumitory (Spring to autumn)

Centaury (Summer)

Black Knapweed (Summer)

Red clover (Spring to autumn)

Bistort (Summer to autumn)

Common vetch (Spring to autumn)

Field scabious (Summer to autumn)

Eyebright (Spring to autumn)

Scarlet pimpernel (Spring to autumn)

Common poppy (Spring to autumn)

These wild flowers all grow in fields and meadows, or along the roadsides. Fields in which animals graze do not contain many wild flowers. Only the grasses and a few tough plants can stand the constant nibbling. Meadows, in which the grasses are allowed to grow higher for hay, contain more flowers. But the best places for grassland flowers are open hillsides and roadside banks. A few flowers, such as the poppy, like soil that has been ploughed. They often grow as weeds in corn fields.

have bigger leaves than plants that grow in the open. The plants in shady places are often taller as well.

The flowers of one kind of plant may be different sizes, but they are almost always made up in the same way. Look first for the number of *petals* – most flowers have four, five, or six. Sometimes they are all alike; sometimes they have different shapes. In some flowers they are joined together to make a tube. Flowers that have similar parts are grouped into families.

What Flowers Are For

The job of the flower is to produce *seeds*, from which new plants can grow. Seeds develop from the *ovules* in the *carpels* after the flower has been pollinated. Pollination means the moving of pollen from the *stamens* to the *stigmas*. Wind or insects usually carry pollen from one flower to another. You should not pick too many wild flowers. If you do, there will not be enough seeds to make new plants for the future.

Above: The primrose is a sure sign of spring. It flowers in woodlands and along hedgerows.

Below: Some flowers of fields and meadows.

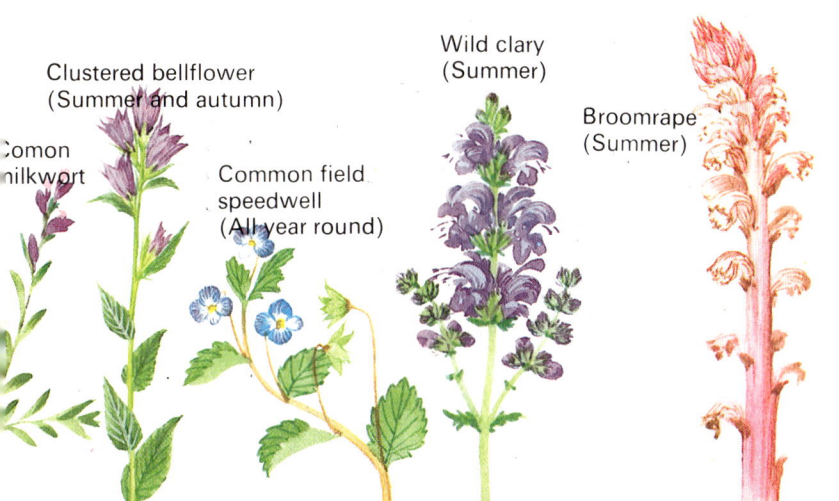

Clustered bellflower (Summer and autumn)

Common milkwort

Common field speedwell (All year round)

Wild clary (Summer)

Broomrape (Summer)

Cowslip (Spring and early summer)

Bulbous buttercup (Spring and early summer)

Birdsfoot trefoil (Summer)

Fire from the Earth

Dots show where most volcanoes rise. There are more than 450 active volcanoes on land and another 80 below the sea. So many of these fiery mountains rim the Pacific Ocean that people talk about them as a Ring of Fire. Many of the world's extinct volcanoes are not shown on this map.

Deep down beneath the solid ground lies rock so hot that it can creep about like melted, sticky tar. Some of this molten rock escapes from cracks and holes. These are volcanoes. Molten volcanic rock cools and hardens in the open air. It piles up around the mouth of a volcano as a thick layer of volcanic rock or builds a volcanic mountain peak. Most volcanoes grow where molten rock escapes from places where the Earth's hard, rocky crust is weak.

Quiet and Violent Volcanoes

There are three main kinds of volcano. Each erupts in a different way. Some erupt quietly. Others are explosive. Yet other volcanoes are in-between.

Quiet volcanoes ooze molten rock. This is called lava where it reaches the surface. Runny lava may spread for miles before it cools and hardens. Lava of this kind builds hills or mountains that slope gradually from the mouth of the volcano. The largest quiet volcano is Mauna Loa in the Hawaiian Islands. Measured from its base beneath the sea, Mauna Loa is the world's largest and highest mountain.

Explosive volcanoes throw out rocks mixed with gas that has been trapped underground. The escaping gas hurls hot ashes and lumps of red-hot lava high in the air, like bullets fired from a gun. When the ash falls it piles up to build a steep-sided mountain shaped a bit like an ice-cream cone.

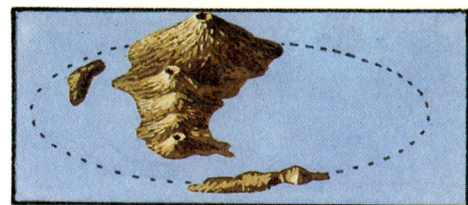

The Krakatoa islands before 1833.

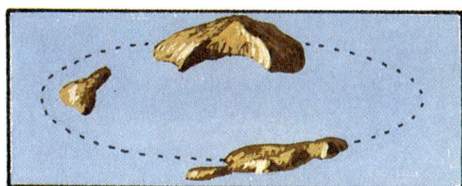

After the 1883 explosion.

Anak Krakatoa

In 1833 the volcanic island of Krakatoa blew up with the force of many atom bombs. A giant sea wave drowned 36,000 people on nearby Indonesian islands. In 1920 Anak Krakatoa (child of Krakatoa) peeped up where Krakatoa used to stand.

Plaster poured into hollows in volcanic ash formed the shapes of a dog and two people. These all died 2000 years ago when Mt. Vesuvius erupted, and buried the Roman town of Pompeii with ash.

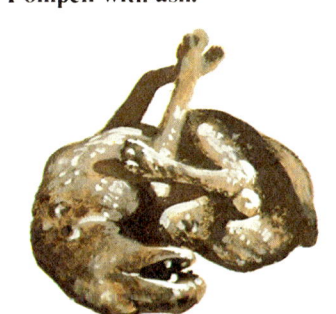

Smoke and flames rise from the island of Surtsey. This was born when a volcano grew out of the sea near Iceland in 1963. First the sea boiled. Then a heap of hot cinders rose above the waves. Many islands of the open ocean began in just this way.

Dangerous and Safe Volcanoes

Explosive volcanoes may erupt without warning. This can be very dangerous for people living nearby. In 1902 about 30,000 people died when a cloud of hot, poisonous gas rolled down Mt. Pelée in the West Indian island of Martinique. In the whole town of St. Pierre just one man escaped alive. He was a criminal locked in a deep prison.

Even in-between volcanoes can be dangerous. At quiet times they ooze lava. At explosive times they shoot out gas and ash. In-between volcanoes build mountains made of layers – ash, then lava, then ash, and so on.

Volcanoes that lie quiet are called dormant. Volcanoes that stopped erupting thousands of years ago are said to be extinct. Edinburgh Castle in Scotland stands on the remains of an extinct volcano.

The World of SCIENCE

The Fiery Sun

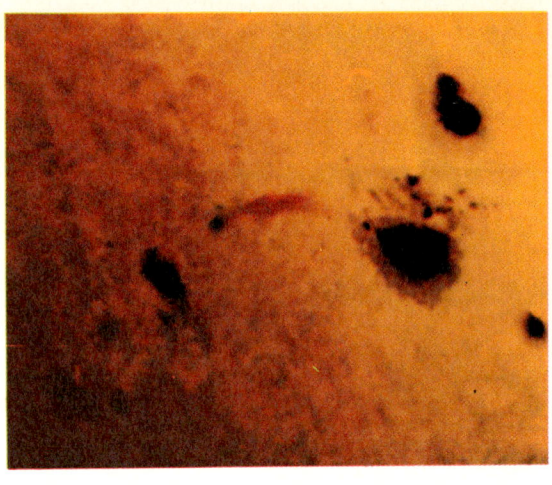

Without our friendly Sun there would be no life on Earth. Without its light and heat, the Earth would be a cold lifeless lump of rock.

The Sun is a huge fiery ball of gas, a hundred times bigger than the Earth. Even although it is made of gas, it contains 750 times more material than the rest of the solar system put together. At its blazing surface the temperature is 6000°C (iron melts at 1530°C). But at the Sun's centre the temperature rises to 15 million degrees, a heat so great that it is quite impossible to imagine it. At the centre, huge atomic explosions are constantly taking place – explosions much greater than any hydrogen bomb explosion on Earth. It is these explosions that give the Sun its light and heat.

The Strange Sunspots

Dark patches called "sunspots" are often seen on the face of the Sun. These spots are areas of cooler gas which do not glow as brightly as the rest of the surface. Sunspots can be enormous. Most of them are larger than the Earth.

The number of sunspots that can be seen at any time varies. Every 11 years there is a period with lots and lots of spots. Five years later there are very few. Then they start to build up again. No one knows why this happens, but scientists believe that sunspot activity affects our weather on Earth.

Whatever you do, don't look at the Sun. Doing this can seriously hurt your eyes.

Storms on the Sun

The Sun's face is often marked by storms. These storms, known as *flares*, throw off parts of atoms which travel through space and can cause interference with our radios on Earth.

From time to time, giant looping arches of fiery gas, called *prominences*, are thrown out from the Sun's surface. These can be several hundred thousand kilometres high.

How Long Will the Sun Shine?

The Sun has been shining as it does now for at least 5000 million years. It should go on shining for another 5000 million. Then all its fuel will be used up and it will begin to die.

Above: Sunspots are marks like ink blots on the Sun's face. They show up dark because they are cooler than the rest of the Sun's surface. Spots bigger than the Earth may last for months, others only for hours. The number of sunspots reaches a peak every 11 years.

Right: Part of the Sun has been cut away to show the extremely hot centre. It is in this centre that all the Sun's great energy is made. At the surface you can see huge prominences shooting out into space.

Below: When the Moon hides the Sun in a total eclipse, we can see the outer atmosphere of the Sun called the *corona*. Usually we cannot see this because of the Sun's blinding light.

The planets were born about 4700 million years ago. They began as a vast cloud of gas and dust whirling round the Sun in space. Slowly, over millions of years, the specks of dust in the cloud collided and stuck together. They built up into lumps of material. Gravity pulled these lumps of rock and metal together to form the planets (below). There may be planets whirling around other stars out in space, but they are too faint for us to see with our present telescopes. Astronomers think that one day they may be able to spot other planets, perhaps with the help of big telescopes in space. There may even be another planet like Earth on which living creatures exist.

The Sun's Family

The Sun's family is called the "solar system". There are 9 planets in the solar system: Mercury, Venus, Earth, Mars, Jupiter, Saturn, Uranus, Neptune and Pluto. Some of the planets have smaller moons moving around them.

As the Sun travels through space, it takes its family with it. Each planet is held in position by the attraction, or gravity, of the Sun. If you swing a ball around your head on a piece of string, the string stays tight and the ball always stays the same distance from you as long as you keep swinging it. The speed of the ball keeps it in position. The same thing happens with the planets. They speed around the Sun, held in *orbit* by the pull of the big, fiery ball.

Years and Days
The closer a planet is to the Sun, the hotter it is and the less time it takes to go round the Sun. The time a planet takes to circle the Sun once is its year. Earth takes $365\frac{1}{4}$ days – an Earth year.

Mercury, which is closest to the Sun, takes only

Above you can see the 9 planets of the solar system: Mercury, Venus, Earth, Mars, Jupiter, Saturn, Uranus, Neptune and Pluto. Mercury is closest to the Sun; Pluto is usually farthest away. Some of the planets have their own moons.

The Sun is a star. What is the difference between a planet and a star? A planet is a body that does not give out light of its own. The planets of the solar system all shine by reflecting light from the Sun. We need a telescope to see the planets beyond Saturn.

88 Earth days. It is very hot on Mercury.

On far away Pluto a year lasts for 248 Earth years. Pluto is hardly warmed by the Sun at all.

Each planet spins around on its axis too. The Earth's axis is an imaginary line through the Earth from North Pole to South Pole. As the planet spins, the Sun shines on different parts of its surface. One complete spin is a day. An Earth day lasts 24 hours. Venus spins much more slowly. A day on Venus lasts for 243 Earth days. Venus is a hot planet, hidden by thick clouds. Earth-like animals could not live on this planet because there is no oxygen for them to breathe. In fact, we know of no planet with air like ours.

Mars, the Red Planet

Mars is probably more like Earth than any of the other planets. For many years people wondered whether there could be life on Mars. Some even thought they could see canals criss-crossing its surface. Like Earth, Mars has seasons. At its north and south poles are ice caps which melt in summer.

Now that space probes have visited Mars, we know that there are no canals and no plants. There are probably no living things of any kind. Mars is a rocky desert. Huge dust storms blow across the planet, making the sky look pink and the sunsets purple.

The Giant Planets

The four outer giant planets are Jupiter, Saturn, Uranus and Neptune. They are all cold, unfriendly worlds. Jupiter is the largest planet in the solar system. It is mostly gas and ice, and it is torn by fierce storms. There is a big red spot on its surface. This huge spot is a spinning whirlpool of cloud.

Saturn is circled by beautiful rings. These rings are made up of tiny moonlets circling the big planet. Saturn's rings are 275,000 kilometres from rim to rim. But from top to bottom they are only about 10 kilometres thick. Seen edge on, they are almost invisible.

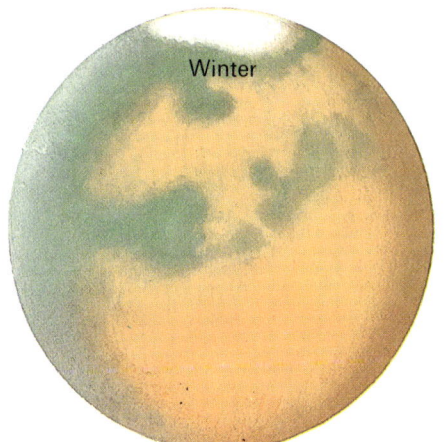

Mars has polar ice caps. They change with the seasons.

87

Our Planet Earth

Our planet Earth is just one of 9 planets that go round and round the Sun. The Earth seems to us to be a big place, but it is only a tiny speck in space. The giant ball of the Sun is a million times bigger than the Earth.

Earth speeds around the Sun at about 18.5 miles per second. It takes Earth $365\frac{1}{4}$ days to go right round the Sun once – a year.

Inside the Earth

The ground that we walk on and all the rocks and mountains that we can see are only a very thin skin on the outside of the Earth. This skin is called Earth's "crust".

The rather light rocks of the crust float on the hotter, heavier rocks underneath. The rocks underneath are called the "mantle".

Below the mantle lies another layer called the "outer core". Scientists think it is made of very hot, molten material, mostly iron and nickel.

Then, right at the centre of the Earth, lies the "inner core". It is probably made of metal.

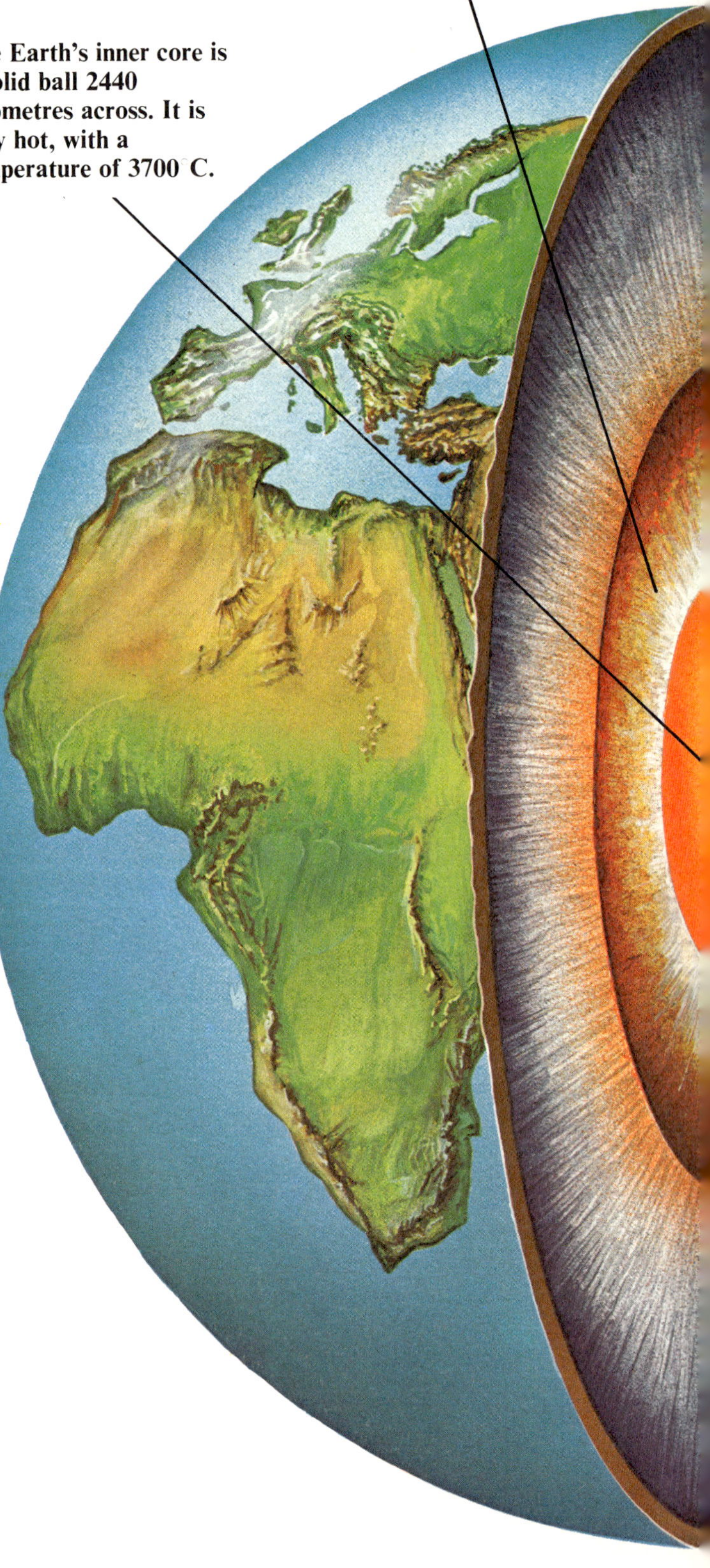

The diagram below shows why it is warmer round the middle of the Earth than at the North and South Poles. At the North and South Poles the Sun's rays have to pass through a greater thickness of atmosphere. The rays are also spread over a larger area. Round the middle of the Earth, at the equator, the Sun's rays come straight down.

The outer core is made of molten metals, mostly iron and nickel.

The Earth's inner core is a solid ball 2440 kilometres across. It is very hot, with a temperature of 3700 C.

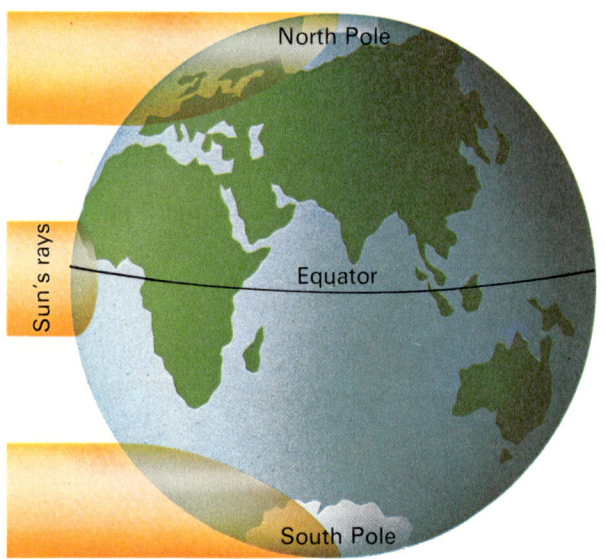

North Pole

Sun's rays

Equator

South Pole

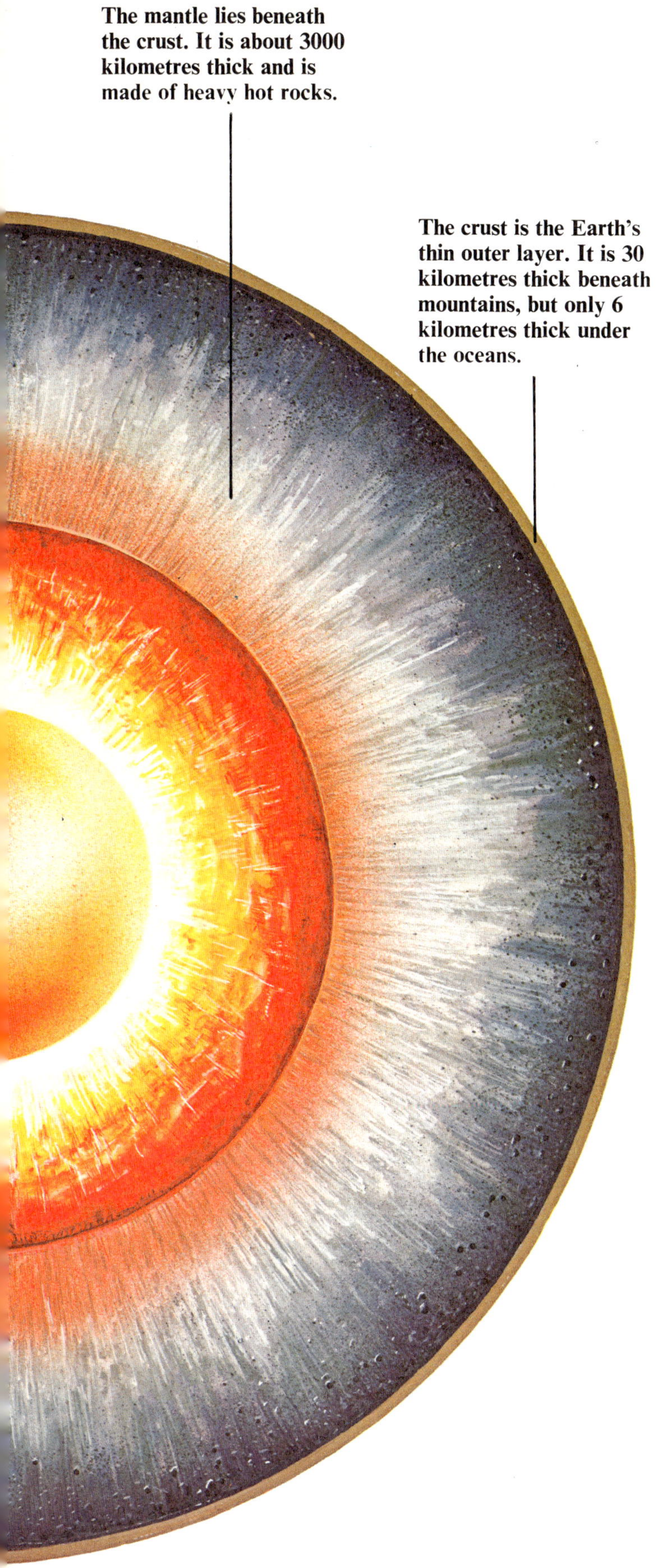

The mantle lies beneath the crust. It is about 3000 kilometres thick and is made of heavy hot rocks.

The crust is the Earth's thin outer layer. It is 30 kilometres thick beneath mountains, but only 6 kilometres thick under the oceans.

The Ice Ages

There have been several great Ice Ages in the Earth's history. The last one began about 600,000 years ago and ended about 15,000 years ago. Fifteen thousand years is not very long in the Earth's history. The Earth was formed about 4500 million years ago.

During the Ice Age great masses of ice spread over large parts of the Earth. The picture above shows how much of the northern part of the world was covered by ice. In places the ice was so thick that the tallest skyscrapers would have been buried deep beneath it.

The Ice Carved Out the Land

In the time of the Ice Age, the world's high mountain ranges were capped by deep snowfields. From these snowfields, great icy glaciers spread out down the foothills to the plains below. These huge slowly-moving rivers of ice carved out wide valleys – most of the valleys we see throughout Europe today.

The ice sheet advanced four times across Europe and North America during the Great Ice Age. In between, there were warmer spells when the ice melted back. Some scientists think that we are now in one of those warmer spells.

Our Moon

The Moon is the Earth's satellite and its nearest neighbour in space. We know more about it than about any other heavenly body. It is so close (about 385,000 kilometres) that you can see things on its surface with your bare eyes. The light areas are rugged highlands. The dark areas are flat, low-lying plains. Everywhere, especially in the highlands, there are great holes, or craters. You can see these clearly in the picture.

The Moon's Phases

The Moon not only changes position from night to night, it also appears to change shape. The Moon has no light of its own. Moonlight is merely light from the Sun being reflected off the Moon's surface. As it goes round the Earth, more or less of the Moon's surface is lit up by the Sun. This causes the different *phases* we see, from new Moon to full Moon, and back to new Moon. From one new Moon to the next new Moon takes $29\frac{1}{2}$ days.

The Moon is an Unpleasant Place

Telescopes, manned landings and lunar probes have told us much about the Moon. We know that it is a most unpleasant place for human beings. It has no air to breathe, no water, no plants or animals. Its days are roasting hot – the temperature at noon is 100°C. Its nights are freezing cold – at midnight it is minus 150°C.

The Moon's Craters

Everywhere you look on the Moon there are craters. Some are tiny; others are vast holes more than 3000 metres deep and 200 metres across. Nearly all of these craters were gouged out when meteorites struck the surface of the Moon. So many meteorites have hit the Moon that they have largely broken up its surface. In places the surface is metres deep in rock chips, dust and tiny grains of glass.

Scientists think that the Earth and our Moon were formed about the same time – 4600 million years ago.

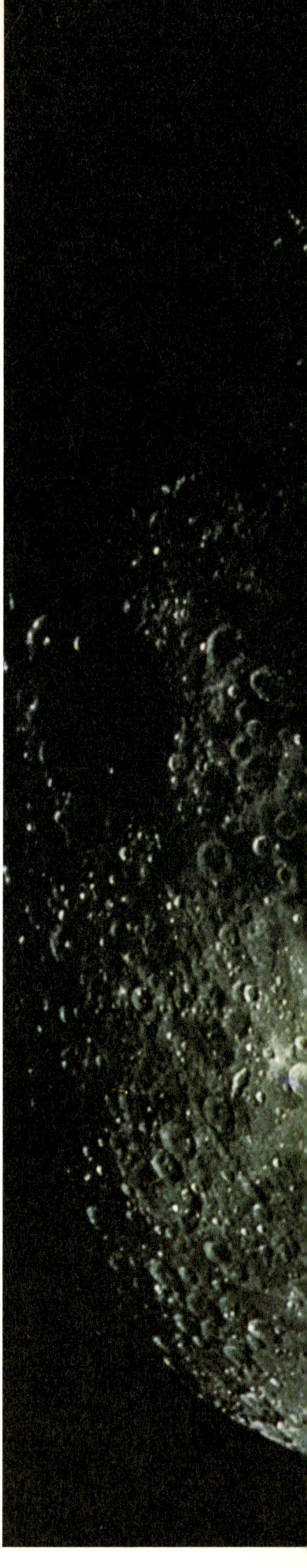

Left: The Moon is really quite small. It only looks as big as the Sun because it is very much closer to us. It is only 3476 kilometres across from edge to edge, one quarter of the Earth's size. The picture shows that the distance across Australia is a little greater than the distance across the Moon.

Under the Sea

Three-quarters of the world is covered by ocean. You can sail in a fast ship across the ocean for days without seeing any land. We talk about the Pacific Ocean, the Atlantic Ocean, the Indian Ocean and the Arctic Ocean. But they all mix together in one great world ocean. The Pacific Ocean alone covers almost a third of the globe. It is larger than all the world's land put together.

The ocean is also very deep. In places it is more than 10 kilometres deep. If Mount Everest was put into the deepest part of the Pacific Ocean there would be nearly 2 kilometres of water over the great mountain's summit.

The Undersea Landscape

The land beneath the ocean is very much like the dry land we know. It has flat plains, valleys and mountains.

Around the edges of the continents are shallow shelves a few kilometres to several hundred kilometres wide. This is the *continental shelf*. You can see it in the picture, the shallow piece of sea next to the land. It is here that most of our fish are caught.

The Deep Ocean

The gentle slope of the continental shelf stops suddenly at the *continental slope*. This plunges steeply down to the real ocean floor. (You can see this in the picture too.) The ocean floor is usually fairly level and is about 3000 to 6000 metres deep. Here and there on the floor are deep trenches. (You can see these in the foreground of the picture.)

Underwater Mountains

Under the oceans there are great ranges of underwater mountains. Sometimes the tops of these mountains stick up above the water as islands. These mountains are often volcanoes.

There is a vast range of mountains running all the way up the middle of the Atlantic ocean. Iceland is at the top of the range and the small island of Tristan da Cunha is at the bottom.

The Ocean's Water

Sea water contains all kinds of substances dissolved in it. About three-quarters of this dissolved substance is common salt. There is enough salt in the world's oceans to cover all the continents to a depth of 150 metres. People have been getting salt from sea water for thousands of years. The water is pumped into shallow pools. Sun and wind evaporate the water until only salt crystals are left.

Magnesium and bromine are two other substances extracted from sea water. Magnesium is a metal that is mixed with other metals to make light, strong materials. Bromine is a chemical used in medicine, photography and motor fuel.

Why Things Fall

Hold a ball at arms length and let it go. It will fall to the ground. Have you ever wondered why the ball falls down instead of up, or sideways.

It is said that a very famous man called Isaac Newton was sitting one day in an orchard. An apple fell from a tree and bounced off his head. As Newton rubbed his head he began to wonder why the apple had behaved as it did. Why did the apple fall down?

We Rely on Gravity

Isaac Newton decided that the Earth and the apple were attracted to each other. But since the Earth is so big, it is not affected by the tiny pull of the apple. The apple is pulled towards the Earth.

The force that pulls the apple towards the Earth is called *gravity*. Gravity pulls everything in the universe towards every other thing. It makes water and bicycles run downhill. It keeps everything on Earth from flying off into space.

And it is the strange pull of gravity that keeps the Earth on its path around the Sun. It also keeps the Moon on its monthly journey round the Earth. If there was no force of gravity, the Earth would fly off into outer space. So would the Moon.

Fighting Gravity

When a spaceship takes off, it uses a huge amount of fuel to push it away from Earth. This fuel is used to fight against the pull of gravity between the spaceship and Earth.

But once the spaceship is away from Earth, the pull of gravity grows less and less. When the spaceship is halfway to the Moon there is hardly any gravity at all. The spacemen float about in their spaceship, not knowing which is up and which is down. They are weightless.

When we weigh things on our kitchen scales we are measuring the force of gravity between the Earth and things like sugar and flour.

People used to think that heavy things fall faster than light ones. But the Italian scientist Galileo showed this was not so. Two balls of the same size but of quite different weights will fall to the ground at exactly the same speed. A bag of feathers would fall at the same speed as a heavy weight if there was no air to affect the bag of feathers' fall.

The skyjumpers in the picture will fall faster and faster when they leave their aircraft. But after a while their speed of fall will not increase because of the air. They may reach a speed of over 300 kilometres an hour before they open their parachutes.

The Power of Steam

Steam Engines

Three centuries ago people only had the power of muscles, wind or flowing water to work factory machines or move loads about. Such power was weak and unreliable. Then inventors learned to use the power in steam. They heated water in a closed container. The water turned to steam that pushed a piston to and fro. Rods linked the piston to a wheel and turned it. By the 1830s engineers were building steam locomotives that could travel faster than a horse and pull much greater loads. Meanwhile other engineers had been building steam-powered ships. Steam power made travel fast and cheap. At last, millions of people could afford to make long journeys.

The Steam Age

The Steam Age lasted for more than a hundred years. Today, internal combustion engines and electric motors do much of the useful work once done by steam. Yet much of our electricity is actually produced by steam. Turbine blades spun by jets of steam may generate electric current that lights and heats your home.

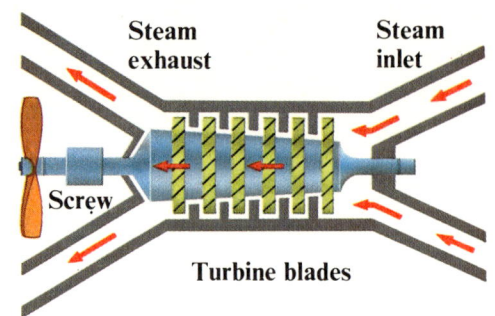

This is the inside of a steam turbine that drives a ship's screw. Steam from two steam inlets rushes past turbine blades fixed to a shaft. The steam turns the blades. These spin the shaft and the screw fixed to one end of it. Used steam escapes through exhaust tubes. In 1897 the early turbine-driven ship *Turbinia* dashed past the Royal Navy at the then amazing speed of $34\frac{1}{2}$ knots (64 k/ph).

Steam locomotives have a boiler made of many tubes that run from end to end. Water for the boiler and coal to heat the water are stored in a tender behind the locomotive. A fireman in the driver's cab feeds coal into a firebox.

Mallard

Mallet

Big Boy

Each of these three steam locomotives has broken a record. The British *Mallard* was the fastest ever. In 1938 it reached 202 km/h on a downhill run. But this speed badly damaged the locomotive's engine. The most powerful steam locomotive ever was an American *Mallet*. This hauled goods trains that measured 2 kilometres from end to end. The largest steam locomotive of all was the Union Pacific *Big Boy*. This weighed more than 500 tonnes with its tender.

Flames and heat are sucked through the locomotive's boiler tubes. These heat the water round them and turn it into steam.

The *Clermont* was the world's first truly successful steamboat. An American named Robert Fulton invented it. A British firm built the engine that drove its paddle wheels. In 1807 the *Clermont* began taking passengers up the Hudson River from New York to Albany. The *Clermont* steamed little faster than many people often walk.

Steam let into cylinders drives pistons to and fro. Connecting rods join the pistons to large driving wheels. Used steam escapes up the chimney. It makes a puffing noise and creates a draught for the fire. Such locomotives scooped up water as they travelled.

Simple Machines

A crowbar (below) is a simple machine. It is a *lever* which lets you lift a heavy weight. It lifts the rock easily because the distance between the block of wood and the rock is shorter than the distance between the block and the end you push down.

A wheelbarrow is a kind of lever too. Its wheel and axle also make up a simple machine. It allows us to move things along the ground much more easily than by dragging them.

A machine is something that helps us do work. Many of today's machines are very complicated, but they are all made up of lots of much simpler machines.

If you try to lift a motor car, you can't. But if you put a jack under one side of it and turn the jack handle, that side of the car rises. The jack is a simple machine that uses the screw to help us lift things easily.

One of the simplest machines is the *wedge* (below left). If we put a wedge in a crack in a piece of wood and hit the wedge with a hammer, the wood will split apart. The wedge being forced into the crack gives a huge outward push. Chisels, knives and axes are all kinds of wedges.

Below right you can see an *inclined plane* – a slope. Pulling a heavy load up a slope takes less effort than lifting it straight off the ground. The inclined plane is really a simple machine.

There are many kinds of levers, some of which we use

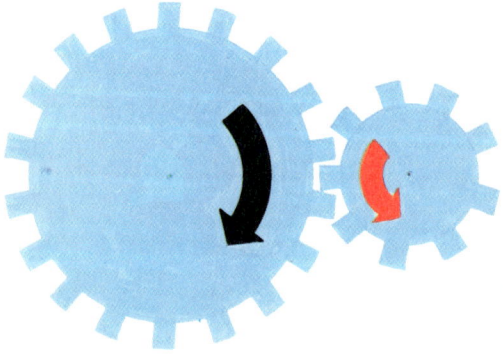

Gears, on the left, are also simple machines. They can help to do work and change speed. If the small wheel with 9 teeth turns once, the big wheel with 18 teeth makes only half a turn. But the turning force of the big wheel is twice that of the small wheel. Bicycles, below, work in the same way. Every time you turn the pedals once, the back wheel goes round several times.

The picture on the left shows a *block and tackle*. It is used to lift very heavy weights. The more wheels that are used in the block and tackle, the easier the lifting is.

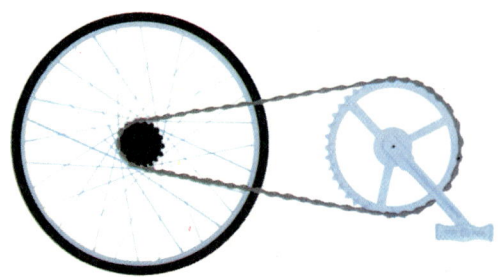

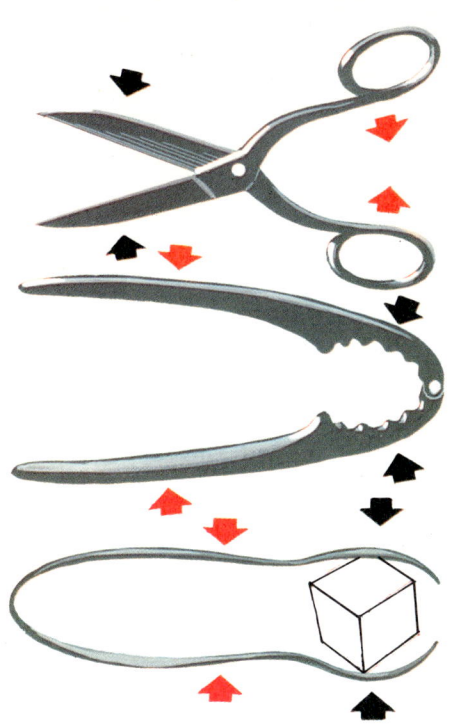

every day. Scissors are levers. They let us use a lot of cutting power without much effort.

Nutcrackers, centre left, are even more powerful levers. A small squeeze at the handle end becomes a large force at the jaws where we put the nuts. But the leverage of the sugar tongs at the bottom on the left is not strong. Can you think why?

Scientists say that work is done when a force moves something. When you pull or lift something you are doing work. Power is the rate at which work is done.

We measure power in things called *watts*. A small electric fire uses electricity at the rate of 1000 watts (1 kilowatt).

One horsepower equals 746 watts, so a horse pulling as hard as it could, would not keep a small electric fire going.

The *pulley* (below) is another simple machine that helps us to lift loads more easily.

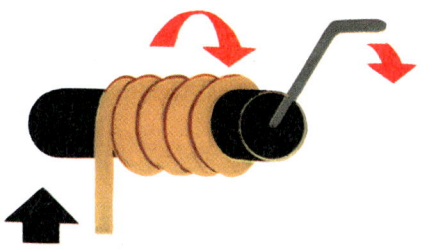

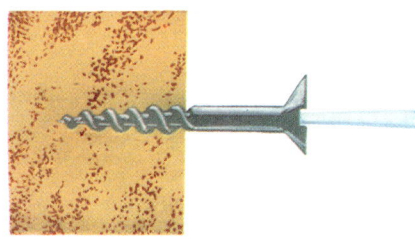

The screw is really a kind of inclined plane. As it turns round and round, the spirals (the *thread*) of the screw pull it into the wood.

The can-opener is another kind of lever. The force at the cutting tip of the opener is much greater than the force you use on the handle.

A *crowbar* can be used for opening crates. It is a simple lever. The longer the handle, the more force you have at the working end.

Here are some more uses for simple machines. Inside more complicated machines such as washing machines, food mixers and vacuum cleaners there are lots and lots of simple machines, all working together.

When we pull a nail out of wood with a hammer like this we are using leverage. It makes the job much easier. You couldn't pull the nail out with your fingers.

A chisel is also a simple lever, rather like the wedge.

All Kinds of Sounds

Listen ... What sounds can you hear? There are sounds all around us. Some are soft, some are loud. But they are all made in the same way, by something moving. Before we can hear a sound, our ears must first pick up sound *waves* travelling through the air.

When something moves, the air vibrates. These invisible vibrations spread out through the air like ripples in a pond. They travel very quickly, at around 340 metres a second.

A World Without Sound

If there were no air, the Earth would be a silent world. Sound waves need air or water or something else to travel through. The Moon is a silent world, because it has no air. Light and radio waves do not need air to travel through. So men on the Moon can use radio to talk to one another.

Our Wonderful Ears

Our ears are wonderful receivers of sound. They catch sound waves travelling through the air. When the sound waves enter the ear, they strike a thin sheet of skin called the *eardrum*. It vibrates, just as a drum does when you hit it.

From the eardrum, the sound waves travel on through three tiny bones until they reach the inner ear. From there they go to the *cochlea*. This is a coiled tube filled with liquid. The liquid vibrates at exactly the same speed as the inner eardrum. The liquid contains tiny hairs that send nerve messages to the brain. The brain tells us we are hearing a sound, and tells us what kind of sound it is.

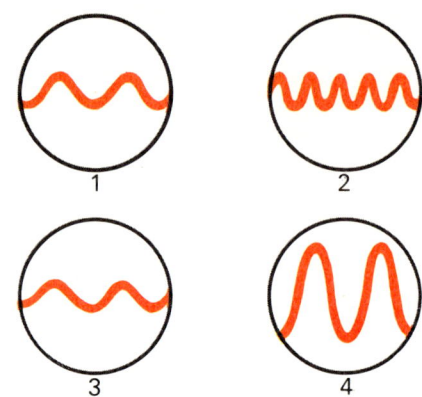

When sound waves go through a microphone, they are changed into electrical waves. We can see this on a screen. Low sounds look rather like picture 1. High sounds look like picture 2. Soft sounds look like 3, and loud sounds look like 4.

Sound waves bounce off things. When a firework goes "bang", some sound goes straight to the man's ear. Other sound waves hit the wall and bounce back. So the man hears an "echo" of the bang.

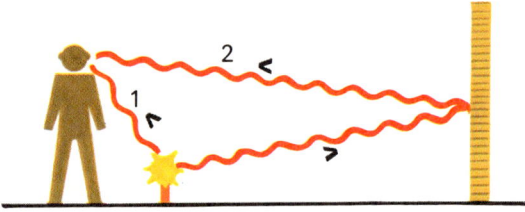

How Ships Use Sound

Ships use "sonar" to measure the depth of the sea. This is how it works. The ship sends out sound signals towards the sea bed. When the sound signals hit the bottom, they bounce back. By measuring the time it takes for the sound to reach the sea bed and bounce back, people on the ship can work out how deep the water is. Sonar is used by warships to find and hunt submarines.

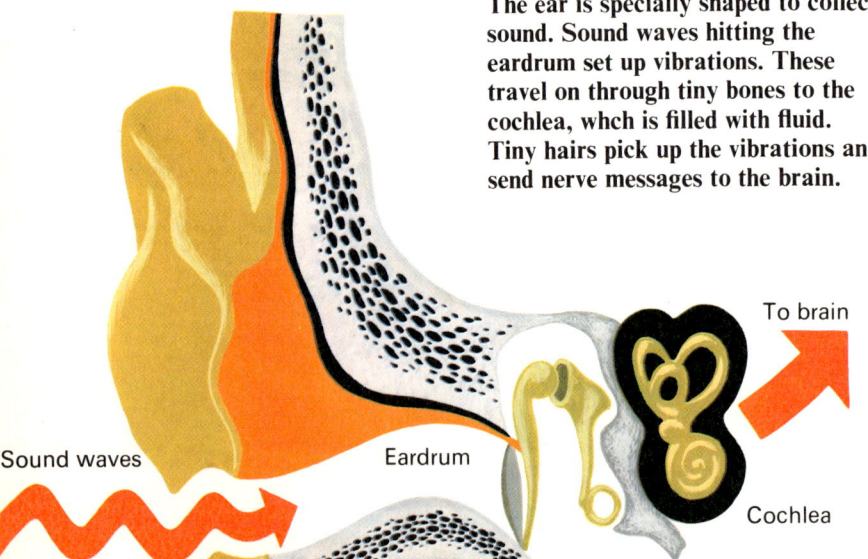

The ear is specially shaped to collect sound. Sound waves hitting the eardrum set up vibrations. These travel on through tiny bones to the cochlea, whch is filled with fluid. Tiny hairs pick up the vibrations and send nerve messages to the brain.

Sound waves   Eardrum   To brain   Cochlea

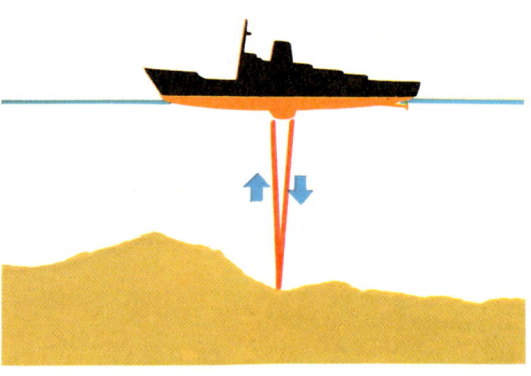

A car horn sounds higher as the car comes nearer – because the sound waves "bunch up" (1). As the car goes away, they stretch out, so the sound is lower (2).

The Concorde is an aeroplane that flies faster than sound. Air gets pushed up in front of the plane. This makes sound waves, which hit the ground, making loud bangs. But the plane is flying so fast that by the time we hear the bang, it is far away.

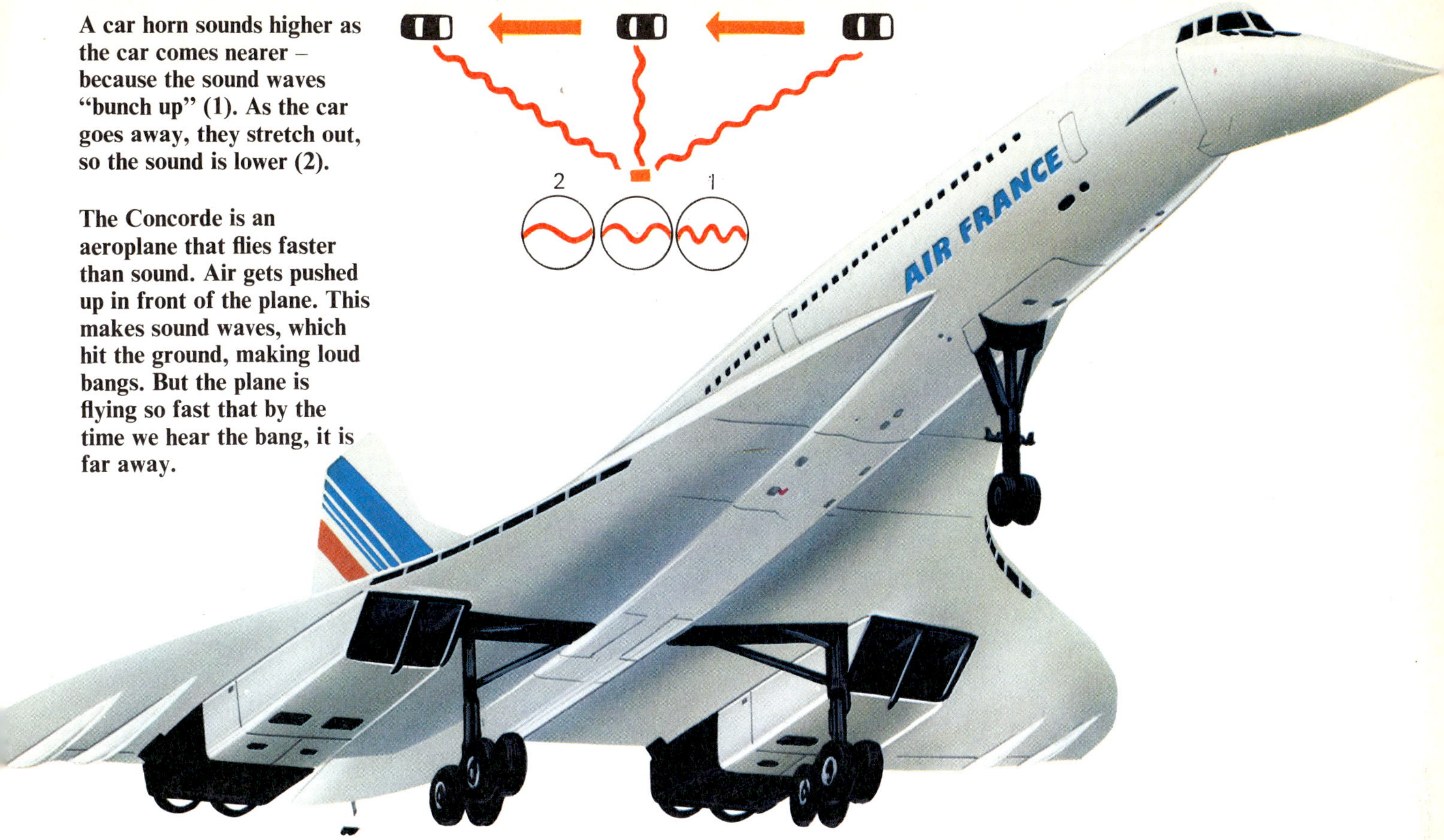

Making Your Own Guitar
You can make your own guitar out of a shoe box. Cut a round hole in the top, as shown in the picture and fasten rubber bands across it with drawing pins. Use rubber bands of different thicknesses if you can. Raise the strings by sliding in a bridge made from card. Play the guitar by gently plucking the strings across the hole.

Moving Through the Air

All sounds are made by movements or vibrations in the air. The faster the vibrations, the higher the sound we hear. The number of sound waves every second is called the *frequency* of the sound. So the faster the vibration, the higher the frequency.

Musical instruments make regular patterns of sounds that are pleasing to hear. A stringed instrument, like the guitar, has strings that vibrate when plucked. When your fingers pluck the strings of a guitar, the body of the guitar also vibrates "in sympathy" with the strings. This is called *resonance*.

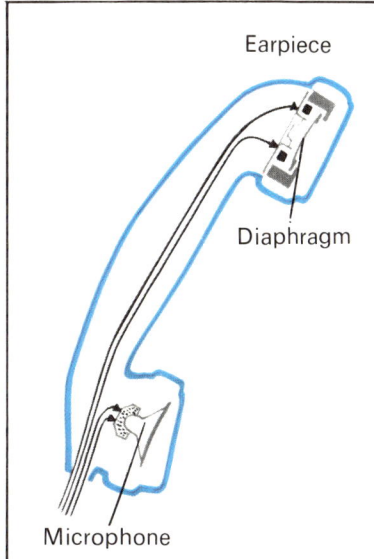

Earpiece

Diaphragm

Microphone

When you talk into a telephone, a microphone vibrates. The sounds are changed into electrical waves and travel through the wires. In the earpiece, they are changed back into sound waves and hit a diaphragm (rather like a drum skin). As this vibrates, the original sounds are copied and the person you are talking to can hear your voice.

Inside a Big Aircraft

Big aircraft were an answer to the problems of increased air travel. More people could travel at once on one plane, and so the numbers of passenger planes in the air could be reduced. That meant that the danger of an overcrowded sky, filled with too many planes, could be avoided.

Of course, bigger planes needed bigger engines as well. Jumbo-jets and airbuses have very powerful engines to lift them into the air and carry them safely on their journeys.

The biggest aircraft can carry hundreds of passengers in comfort, as well as the passengers' luggage and extra freight too. And the number of seats available can be altered to give more room to each seat, and luxury comfort for some.

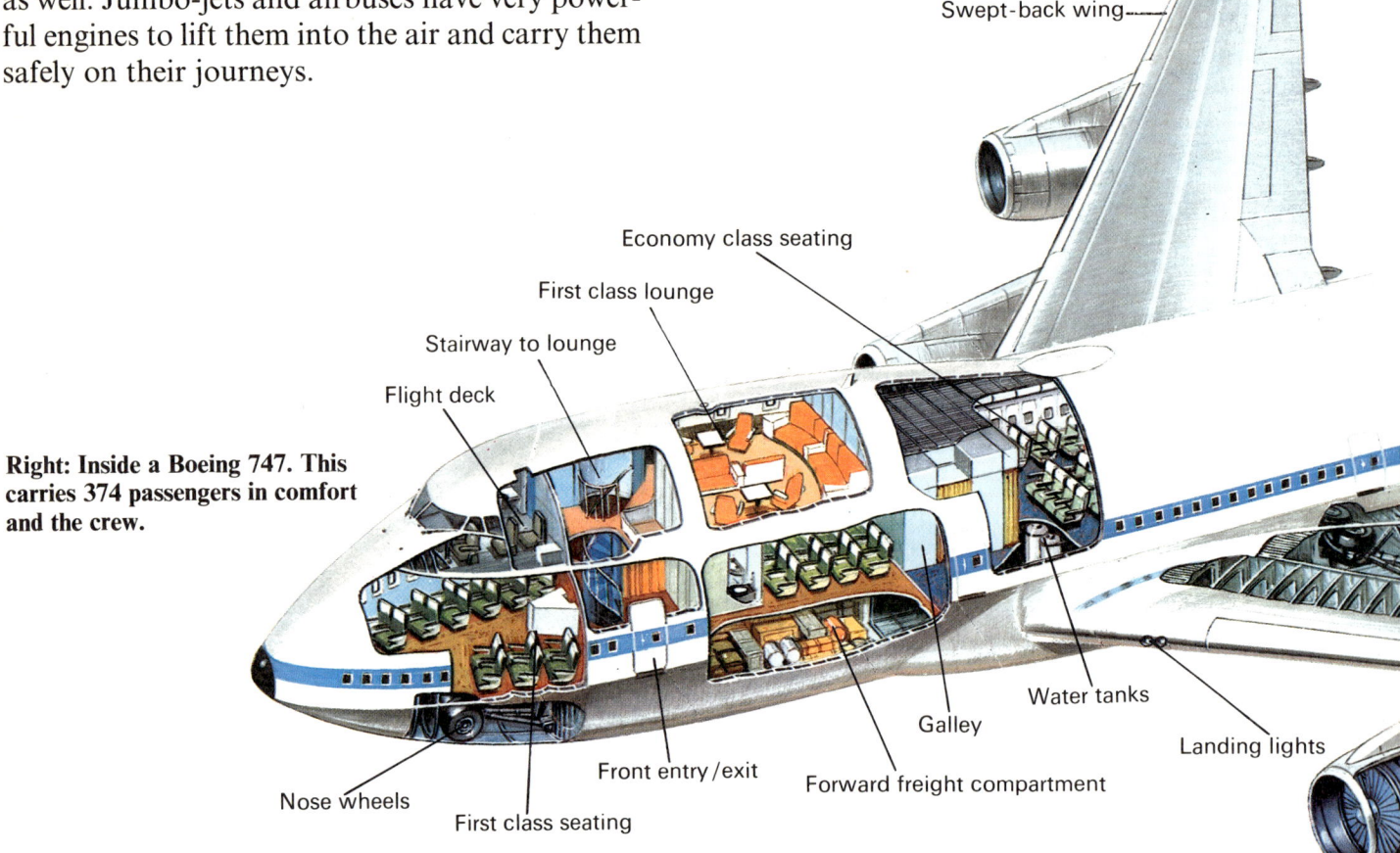

Right: Inside a Boeing 747. This carries 374 passengers in comfort and the crew.

Swept-back wing

Economy class seating

First class lounge

Stairway to lounge

Flight deck

Nose wheels

First class seating

Front entry/exit

Galley

Forward freight compartment

Water tanks

Landing lights

On Board the Jumbos

The first jumbo jet to operate passenger flights was the Boeing 747, in 1970. This was soon followed by the DC-10 and the Lockheed Tristar, but the 747 remains the biggest in terms of the numbers it can carry.

The size of the jumbos, however, has produced some problems for the airlines. In the 1970s, people thought that traffic in the air would keep increasing. But that has not always been true, and many airlines fly their planes with far less people on board than they are built to carry. This means that the airlines lose money on their flights. And when the planes are full, some airports cannot easily cope with so many passengers arriving at the same time.

The Future

No one knows for sure what the future of air travel will be. Supersonic planes like *Concorde* have been brilliantly designed, but they are best for long distance flights, not short ones. And it is still very expensive to fly on *Concorde*, so holiday-makers and ordinary people are not likely to use it.

Short distance flights will probably be taken over by the "airbuses", which are wide-bodied planes now used by many European airlines. Most of these have two or three jet engines, and have room for about 300 people. But the airlines have still to solve the problem of increased fuel costs for their planes, and of filling each flight with people.

Helicopters will be bigger and faster, machines which can land people close to their final destination.

Above: The Boeing 747's flight deck. Modern pilots have computers, navigational aids and an automatic pilot to help them, but they still need to watch all these instruments during the flight.

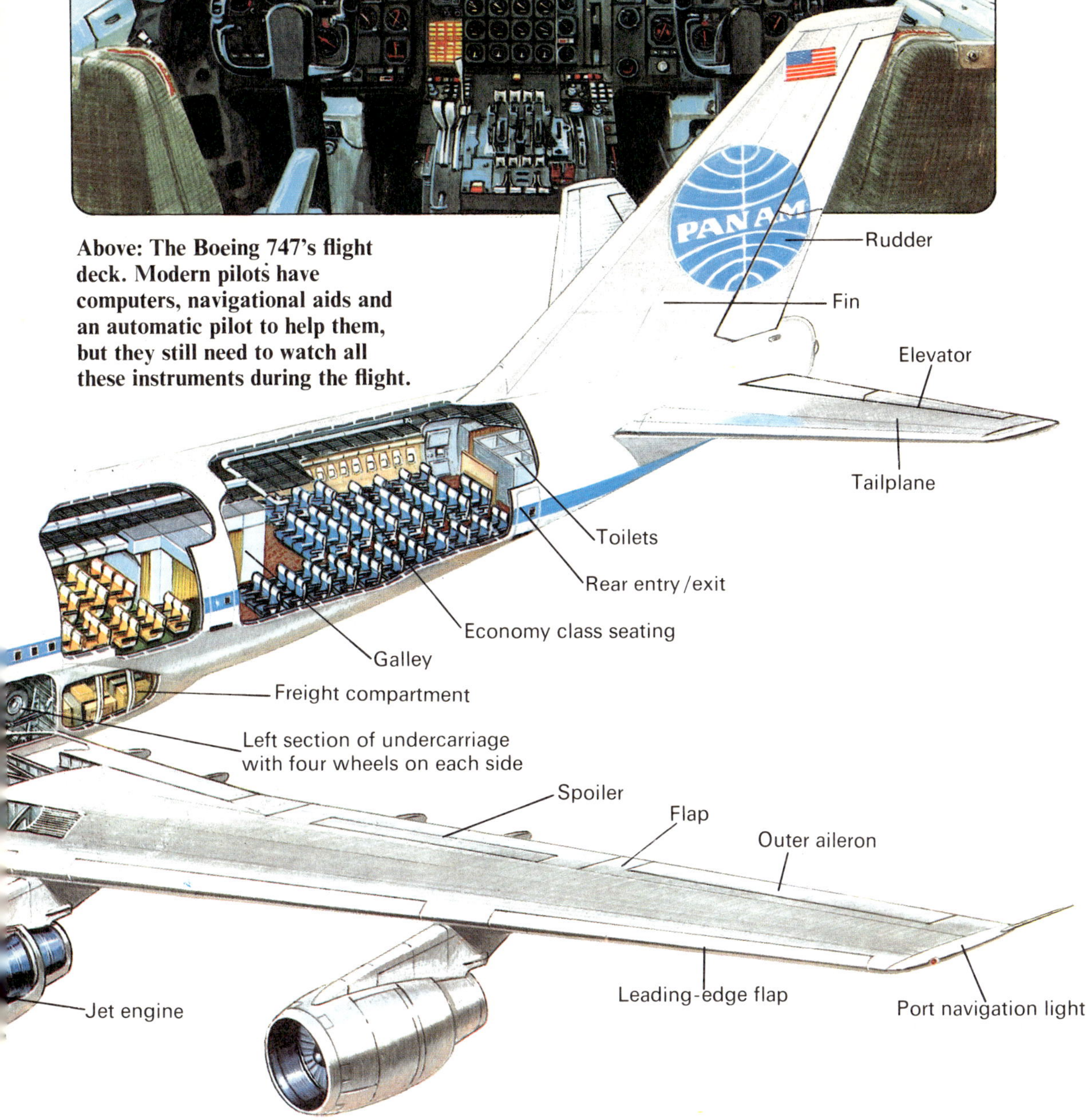

Rudder

Fin

Elevator

Tailplane

Toilets

Rear entry /exit

Economy class seating

Galley

Freight compartment

Left section of undercarriage with four wheels on each side

Spoiler

Flap

Outer aileron

Jet engine

Leading-edge flap

Port navigation light

Concorde taking off. The slim "dart" shaped body is ideal for supersonic flight. It can cruise at over 2000 km/h and seats 140 passengers.

The Story of the Tank

All through history people have had ideas for armoured battle wagons. But it was not until World War I that two British scientists, Tritton and Wilson, began to build a vehicle with thick steel armour that ran on caterpillar tracks. The tracks made it easy to drive over rough ground, where ordinary wheels would slip and skid. In 1916 the world saw its first tanks when 50 Mark Is went into battle. These early tanks were clumsy and slow.

World War II

During World War II the Germans used their Panzer, Panther and Tiger tanks to make lightning attacks into the rest of Europe. But the tank war was won by the American Sherman tanks, the British Churchill tanks and the Russian T-34s. They were produced in tens of thousands. In the end they outnumbered those of the enemy.

After the war, tanks were built which could fight in limited nuclear wars. Many modern tanks can travel under water. They also have an infra-red searchlight so that they can see at night without being seen. (Infra-red rays are like light rays, but they cannot be seen by the human eye.) Many tanks can be carried inside special planes to where they are needed. Today, tank-like armoured personnel carriers have been built which can protect soldiers from radioactive fallout on the battlefield.

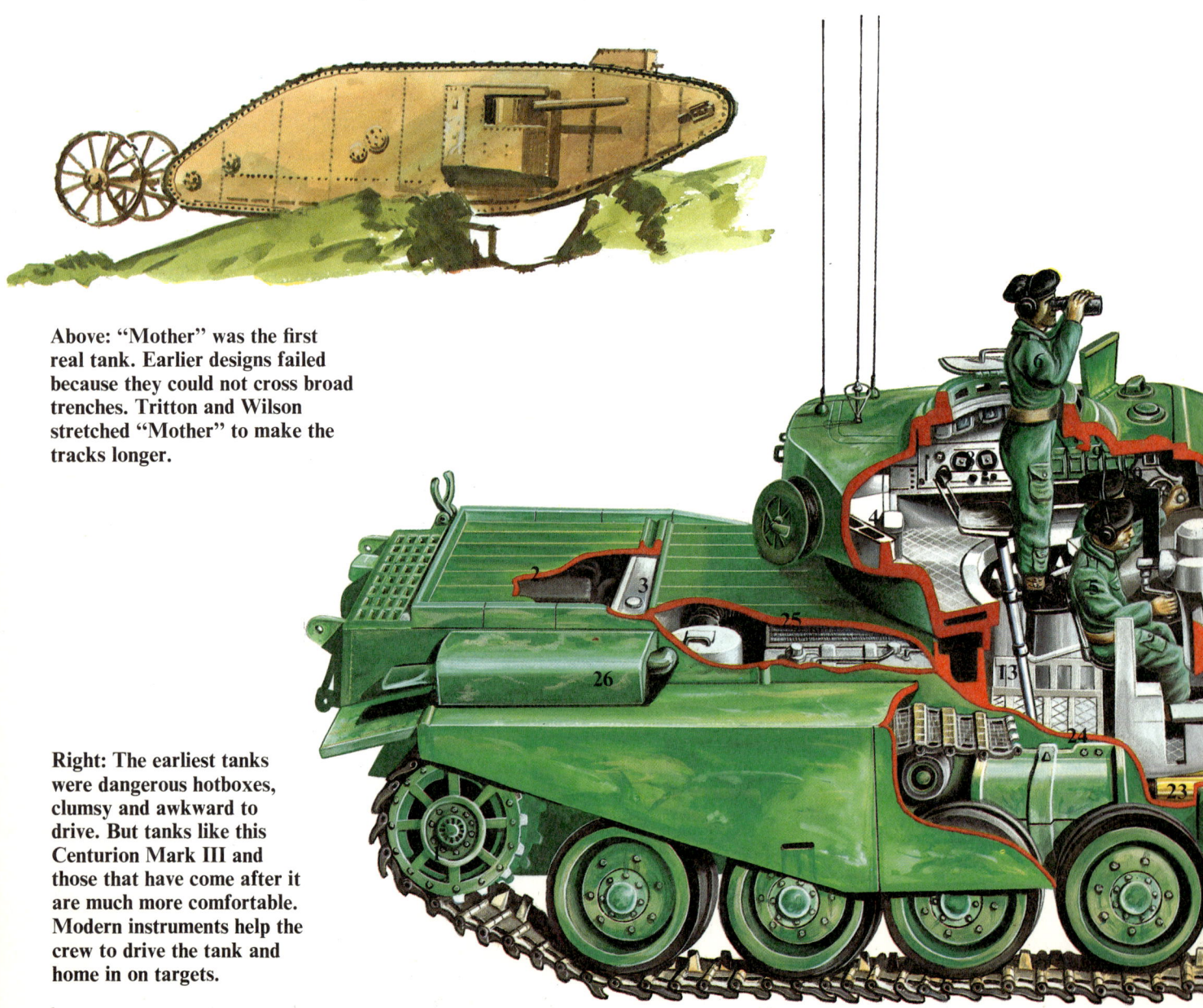

Above: "Mother" was the first real tank. Earlier designs failed because they could not cross broad trenches. Tritton and Wilson stretched "Mother" to make the tracks longer.

Right: The earliest tanks were dangerous hotboxes, clumsy and awkward to drive. But tanks like this Centurion Mark III and those that have come after it are much more comfortable. Modern instruments help the crew to drive the tank and home in on targets.

Above and left: Two tanks of World War II. In 1941, the Russians launched the T34/76 (above) against the Germans. It was one of the best tanks of the war. It weighed 28 tonnes and had 60 mm armour. Germany's Tiger 1E (left) was one of the most powerful tanks of the war. It weighed 56 tonnes, had armour 100 mm thick and carried an 88 mm gun. The great weight of this tank made it difficult to handle.

Right: The modern German Leopard is fitted with a British 105 mm gun. It can travel at fast speeds.

Below: The modern British Chieftain 2, a powerful and reliable tank.

Left: A cutaway view of a British Centurion Mark III tank of 1950, showing the inside with equipment and crew. This tank had an 84 mm gun which could be aimed accurately no matter how the tank moved. (1) Drive sprocket, (2) Engine and transmission, (3) Fuel tanks, (4) Crew storage, (5) Gunner, (6) Commander, (7) Commander's episcope, for looking out of the tank, (8) Radio, (9) Machine-gun ammunition, (10) Loader, (11) 3 in machine-gun, (12) 84 mm main gun, (13) Motor for rotating turret, (14) Muzzle brake, (15) Gunner's information display box, (16) Driver's episcope, (17) Driver, (18) Steering levers, (19) Idler, (20) Turret floor, (21) Road wheels, (22) Gun elevation motor, (23) Main ammunition, (24) Bin for empty shellcases, (25) Radiators, (26) Armoured exhaust.

The Future

Unless the very rapid increase in the number of people in the world slows down, we will have to move into space to find more room to live. There are now about 4500 million people on Earth. By the year 2020 there could be about 10,000 million of us unless people have fewer babies.

The First Space Colonies

First of all, space stations will be put in position a few hundred kilometres above the Earth. These will be the starting point for the next stage in space living – permanent space colonies. The first colonies will probably be about 350,000 kilometres from Earth and nearer to the Moon. Designs for different kinds of space colonies have already been worked out. You can see one at the top of the opposite page.

Material From the Moon

When people are building the first space colonies they will probably get most of their materials from the Moon. Shooting space ships from the Moon is much easier than shooting them off the Earth. This is because the Moon is much smaller and has much less gravity pull.

On to the Other Planets

But building cities between the Earth and the Moon may only be the beginning. People will slowly venture out to the other planets.

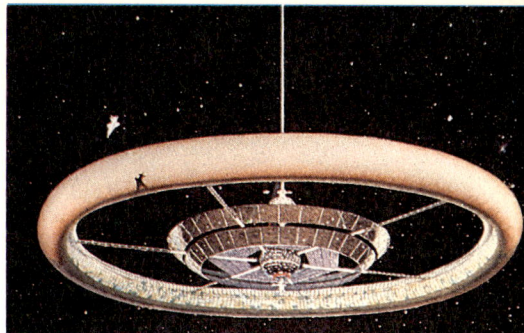

The picture above shows a huge space station of the future. The whole station is made to turn round and round like a giant bicycle wheel. This makes gravity inside the outer rim, where people would live. They will not float about as today's spacemen do. In the centre "hub" of the great wheel are power plants using sunlight, docking stations and mirrors to reflect sunlight into the living areas. The whole wheel will be about 2000 metres across and will go right round once every minute. The outside "tyre" part of the wheel will be 130 metres across. In it will live as many as 10,000 people, with land and water, just as we have on Earth. With constant sunlight, the space colonists will be able to grow several crops a year.

The scene on the left could take place in the year 2050. It shows a base on Phobos, one of the tiny moons of Mars. Slowly but surely people will venture farther and farther afield in space. They will search out places where the human race can go on expanding. To begin with, they may look at Mars which, in some ways, is quite like Earth. The Martian day is nearly the same length as ours, and Mars has seasons too. But there is no life-giving oxygen in the Martian atmosphere, and nothing grows. People will have to take their own air and food with them. When the first base is built on Mars, the colony will grow quite quickly. The first arrivals will be engineers and miners. They will mine raw materials for building in glass and concrete. Giant greenhouses will be built to grow food for the colony. Electricity will be generated in nuclear power plants. After a while the whole of Phobos may become a spaceport – the tiny moon is only 22 kilometres across.

The World of
ART

An Ancient Greek Theatre

Plays and the theatre today are mostly just for fun and entertainment, but when they began in ancient Greece they were a serious part of the worship of the gods. The Greeks held festivals for their gods, and sang and danced stories about them. At first, theatre buildings were not used for this. The audience stood around a patch of ground to watch and listen to the performers. But later, theatres like the one in the picture below were built. The first was built near the temple of the god Dionysus, for plays were still to do with worship, and theatres in Greece were always sacred places.

The early Greek plays were all about the gods and goddesses. A group of actors sang the story together, but sometimes one actor sang alone to tell one part of the story. Later, three actors each had separate parts to play, although there was still a *chorus* of extra actors who told the audience the main parts of the story. No women were allowed to act, and so all the parts were played by men – even those of women and young boys and girls!

In classical Greece the actors all wore masks to show the characters they played. This meant that one solo actor could take many roles.

Visiting the theatre was an important and exciting event for the ancient Greeks. It did not cost much to go, and the plays lasted all day, starting very early in the morning and going on until evening. On most festival days there were at least three plays to watch, and an extra one at the end which was funny. People took food with them, met their friends there and enjoyed themselves together.

You can see from the picture that the theatre stage had different parts. The chorus of actors worked in the ground-level part, and the main actors used the raised platform. The dressing rooms were behind the raised stage, and the main actors changed their masks and costumes there, between scenes. The stone in the middle of the ground-level stage is an altar, from the times when plays were religious events.

Most of the plays were still about gods and goddesses, or about the famous Greek heroes and their adventures. This meant that most of the audience knew the stories in advance, but they still enjoyed finding out what the playwright wanted to tell them about those events.

The theatre began in Athens, but soon spread to other Greek cities too. Soon companies of actors toured everywhere.

Right: Most people in a Greek theatre sat on ordinary stone slabs, but these seats were built for important guests, who sat at the front. You can still see the carefully-carved arm rests on them. They belong to a Greek theatre built in a city which is now part of modern Turkey.

Below: This picture shows what a Greek theatre would have looked like from the very top seats in the audience. The day of plays has just begun, and you can see a queue of late-comers on the road outside.

Buildings, Old and New

When people first made houses to live in, they built them as best they could. They used any materials they could find nearby. But as time went by, they gained skill in building and had more materials to work with. They began to design their buildings before they put them up. We use the word "architecture" to describe this design work.

An Architect's Job

An architect begins his work by finding out what the building is going to be used for. Is it a house for people to live in, a factory or an office? Then he prepares rough sketches and talks about them with the people for whom he is designing the building. When the designs are approved, he makes the final plans. The builders work from these plans.

Ancient Architecture

The people of ancient civilizations had many fine buildings. They must have had skilled architects to design them. The Egyptians built great temples of stone. The people of ancient Babylonia and Assyria used bricks. In India there are ruins of vast buildings of brick and stone.

Some of the finest architecture was that of ancient Greece, dating from the 600s BC. The Greeks built their temples and other buildings with graceful pillars and decorated them with fine sculpture.

The Romans copied the Greek way of building. But they made great use of arches. They designed their houses with baths and central heating, and decorated them with wall paintings and mosaics.

On the right is a picture of New York at night. Skyscrapers like these only became possible when strong steel girders could be used as a framework to the building. And without lifts to carry people up and down inside the buildings, no one would have wanted skyscrapers. Taller and taller buildings will be put up as space on the ground becomes scarcer and scarcer.

Below you can see Roman houses being built. The Romans had large saws for cutting stone into building blocks, and hammers and chisels for decorating the stone. They had huge cranes for lifting heavy weights. You can see one in the background of the picture. The big wheel, turned by men walking inside it, wound the lifting rope around the drum. For lighter loads they used the simple rope and pulley. Roman builders moulded clay and baked it into bricks and tiles. They mixed sand, lime and water to make mortar for joining bricks or plastering walls. You can see a man plastering over a brick column in the picture. Some columns were made of solid blocks of stone, as in the background of the picture. Many of the tools that the Romans used were very like the ones we use today.

Western Architecture

In western Europe a style of building called *Romanesque* developed. It was very solid and heavy. The great Norman churches, such as Durham Cathedral, are Romanesque.

By the late 1100s a lighter, more graceful style which we call *Gothic* grew up. Gothic cathedrals had tall slender pillars, high vaulted roofs and big windows that were often filled with stained glass.

Modern Architecture

New materials such as steel and concrete made many changes in design possible. By using steel frames architects could build much taller buildings. In this way, the skyscrapers of New York and other big cities came into being. They made the best use of small, crowded sites.

Nowadays, concrete with steel inside it can be cast away from the building site. These factory-made sections can then be put together on the site.

Architects now pay more attention to the surroundings of their buildings. They try to make sure that their buildings are not only good to look at, but also pleasant places in which to live.

The Renaissance

Lorenzo de' Medici was a wealthy banker whose family ruled Florence. Their money helped to pay for many great works of art.

Rich men and women of Renaissance times all wore brightly coloured clothes. Wealthy noblemen enjoyed hunting deer and wild boar in the open countryside. They chased stags but left the female deer, or does, alone. Noblemen rode horses, but their huntsmen often ran on foot. Hounds helped to track and tire the quarry. Men killed with spears.

"Renaissance" means being born again. In Italy six hundred years ago people said that painting, music and other arts had come to life again. Of course they had never really died at all. What actually happened was this. Artists, architects and writers discovered half-forgotten ideas from ancient Rome and Greece. Then they used these old ideas in brand new ways.

Rich rulers paid architects to build fine palaces. They paid artists to cover walls with splendid paintings. Meanwhile, thinkers questioned old beliefs about the world. Also, sailors set out to explore it.

The Renaissance began in Italy in the 1300s. By the 1500s it had spread to nearby European lands.

The old woodcut below shows peasants shearing sheep. Such country folk worked long and hard for little pay. Indeed, in those Renaissance times there were even slaves who worked for nothing. Rich Venetians bought slaves in the East. They kept some slaves for doing housework and sold the rest for profit.

SAVOY
Milan
Verona
Venice
Padua
Mantua
Parma
Genoa
GENOA
Bologna
Lucca
Pisa
Florence
Rimini
Urbino
Siena
Assisi
VENETIAN REPUBLIC
CORSICA
PAPAL STATES
Rome
Ostia
KINGDOM OF NAPLES
Naples
SARDINIA
SICILY

Renaissance Italy was divided into many states. These often fought one another. Yet cities like Florence, Rome and Venice grew extremely rich.

Three Famous Painters

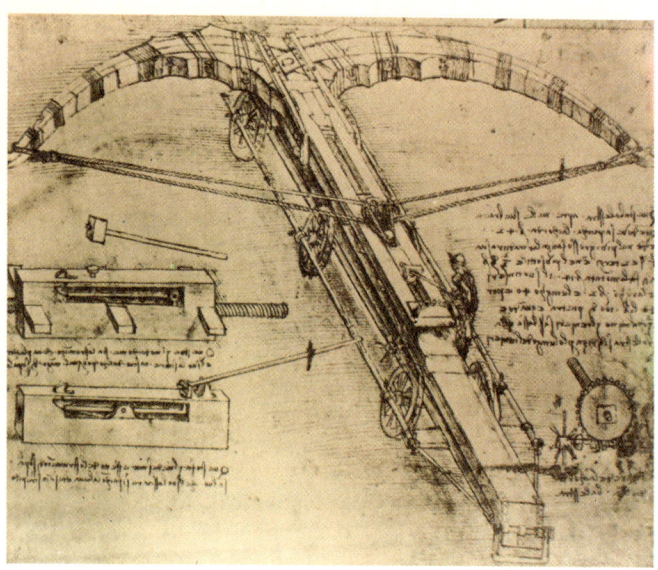

Leonardo da Vinci (1452–1519)

Leonardo was an amazing genius. He was a wonderful painter and sculptor. But he was also a mathematician, a composer of music, a military engineer, an inventor and a scientist.

Leonardo was born near Florence in Italy. He showed such talent at drawing that his father sent him to study with the famous painter Andrea del Verocchio. The pupil soon outshone the teacher. Leonardo's work was in great demand, but he often left paintings unfinished, turning to some new idea. His most famous masterpieces include "The Last Supper" and the "Mona Lisa". Unfortunately, the rich colours of some of his paintings quickly faded, because he was always experimenting with new paints.

As a scientist and inventor, Leonardo was years ahead of his time. He even drew plans for an armoured tank and a helicopter. Because no suitable engine had yet been invented, he never managed to build any of these amazing machines.

Leonardo's inventive brain produced a number of strange war engines. He designed guns with many barrels, explosive mortar bombs, and this giant crossbow, so huge that it rested on a six-wheeled trolley with inclined wheels.

Below: One of Leonardo's most famous paintings, "Virgin and Child with St Anne". The great artist painted this picture in Florence towards the end of his life. Below right: Leonardo drew this portrait of himself in red chalk

Vincent Van Gogh (1853–1890)

Vincent Van Gogh was born in Holland. At first, he wanted to be a preacher but later he turned to painting. He loved to paint scenes of everyday life showing ordinary people.

In 1886 Van Gogh went to live with his brother in Paris. There he met other artists and began to use much brighter colours. He worked very hard, trying to capture the changing scenes of the countryside. Though many of his pictures are sunny, Van Gogh was a very unhappy man. He had no money and he spent some time in a mental hospital. During a spell of madness, he cut off part of his left ear. You can see the self-portrait he painted. Because it was done looking into a mirror, it shows the right ear bandaged.

Even while he was ill, Van Gogh went on painting. In all he made more than 800 oil paintings. Yet he sold only one. In the end, despair overcame him and he killed himself. Today, his paintings are admired everywhere and are sold for huge sums of money.

Picasso painted this picture, called "Woman in a Chemise" in 1905.

Van Gogh's self-portrait, done in 1889, shows his bandaged ear.

Pablo Picasso (1881–1973)

Many great painters died poor and unknown. Picasso, however, became rich and famous during his lifetime. He was admired as the greatest artist of the 20th century, even though people sometimes found his paintings difficult to understand.

Pablo Picasso was born in Malaga, Spain. But he lived for many years in France. When he was a young man, he copied the style of the French "Impressionist" painters. Then, he turned from bright colours to rather sad, still pictures. Because blue was his favourite colour at this time, we call it his "Blue Period".

Later, Picasso gave up painting lifelike figures of people. Instead he drew patterns of shapes, lines and colours. This is called "abstract" painting. Because he drew so many cubes (block shapes) in these pictures, people called Picasso's new style "Cubist". Besides painting, Picasso also made sculptures, collages (pictures made from pieces of wood, paper and cloth), and fine pottery.

Ballet

Ballet is a kind of entertainment that is danced to music. But unlike other types of dancing, ballet follows strict rules. These have been laid down since ballet began at the court of Louis XIV of France in the 1600s. For over 200 years Paris was the centre of the ballet world. Today, all the steps in ballet still have French names.

To create a ballet, a *composer* writes the music and a *choreographer* thinks up the steps and movements the dancers will make. The *designer* decides what the stage set and costumes will look like. Modern ballet, though it gives more freedom to the dancer than traditional, or *classical*, ballet, still follows the same rules.

Right: Janet Bradley dances on her toes *(en pointe)* **in the role of Little Red Riding Hood in** *Sleeping Beauty.*
Below: Piglets dance a *pas de deux* **from** *The Tales of Beatrix Potter*, **a modern ballet. In a** *pas de deux*, **the male dancer supports the ballerina in graceful and difficult movements.**

Above: A graceful scene from *Swan Lake*, one of the popular ballets danced to music by Peter Ilyich Tchaikovsky, the great Russian composer. He also wrote the music for *Sleeping Beauty* and *The Nutcracker*.

Below: Wide leaps in ballet are called *grands jetés*, which means "big jumps" in French. The height to which a dancer rises in the air during a jump is called *elevation*. Good elevation is particularly important for male dancers.

Above: A jump called *changement de pieds* (changing the feet). The dancer's feet change position in the air: if, at the beginning, the right foot is in front, it will be behind on landing.

Right: A junior class at the ballet school in Stuttgart, West Germany. When children join a ballet school at ten or eleven, they have usually had four or five years of dancing lessons.

Three Famous Composers

Few people agree about who was the greatest composer of music. What everyone would agree on is that the three composers we talk about here were among the greatest that ever lived.

Lots of Musical Bachs

Johann Sebastian Bach was born in 1685 in the small town of Eisenach in Germany. He came from a big family and they were all musical. In fact, there were more than sixty musical Bachs before the family died out in the 1800s.

Bach was only 10 years old when his father died. He studied music whenever he could, often creeping out of bed to copy music from his eldest brother's collection. He was so keen on music he once walked to Hamburg, 240 kilometres away, to hear a great organist play.

The Great Composer

Bach worked tirelessly, composing music for the Church and for rich German princes who employed musicians to entertain them. Many of his greatest pieces of music were written for the organ or for singing.

When Bach died in 1750 his music was almost forgotten. About a hundred years passed by before people began to realize what a genius Johann Sebastian Bach had been.

A Boy Genius

Six years after Bach died, Wolfgang Amadeus Mozart was born in the beautiful city of Salzburg. Mozart's father taught him music from a very early age. By the time he was four the young Mozart was found with a piece of paper covered with inky scribbles. He said that he was writing a concerto. To everyone's amazement he sat down at the harpsichord and played what he had written. By the time he was 7, Mozart was playing in concerts all over Europe.

Below left: Bach was a great organist. Here he is playing on the simple organ of the church in Arnstadt, where he was in charge of the choir.

Below: A splendid organ built in a church in Dresden during Bach's lifetime. This kind of organ can play several tunes at once.

Left: A bronze bust of Beethoven. It was based on a mask of the composer made in 1812. It is the best likeness we have of the great man.

Right: The seven-year-old Mozart with his father and sister.

He Died a Poor Man

Mozart wrote over 600 pieces of music, including many beautiful operas and symphonies. But he earned little money for all his hard work. He died a poor man when he was only 35.

Another Musical Genius

When Mozart died in 1791, Ludwig van Beethoven was 21 years of age. The two great composers had met in 1787. Then Beethoven played for Mozart, and Mozart was very impressed.

Beethoven was born in Bonn, now the capital of West Germany. His father taught him to play the

Mozart was 6 years old when this picture was painted. He is dressed in a gold-braided suit given to him by the Empress of Austria. The young Mozart played for the Empress, who made a great fuss of him.

piano and the violin. By the time he was 11 he was playing in concerts. Shortly afterwards he was made assistant court organist at Bonn.

Beethoven Fights his Deafness

Beethoven had a piece of piano music published when he was 12 years old. Before long he was famous both for his piano playing and for the music he composed.

In 1792 Beethoven went to Vienna in Austria. There he had lessons from another famous composer, Joseph Haydn.

When he was only 26 years old Beethoven found that he was going deaf. But he told no one until about five years later. In spite of this handicap, he went on playing and composing. Some of his finest music, including three of his nine great symphonies, were written when he was almost completely deaf. Even when he was totally deaf, Beethoven went on composing. He heard the music only in his mind. All he could do to help his hearing was to use ear trumpets. Today, a simple operation or a hearing aid would probably have been able to cure the great man's deafness. He died in Vienna in the year 1827.

The Crafts

Since the time of the Stone Age, crafts have been important in people's lives. Skilful ways of making things by hand, such as pots, carpets or baskets, have been passed down from generation to generation.

Fine decoration and beautiful design in ordinary everyday things are signs of a civilized people.

On these two pages you can see pictures of some fine objects made by master craftsmen. They come from different parts of the world and were made in different centuries, but they are all pleasing to look at.

The ancient Greeks were famous for their beautiful pottery work. The pot above shows a master potter at work. It was made about 5000 years before Christ.

The Egyptians made statues in gold to bury with their dead pharaohs. Master craftsmen were employed to make these statues. The one on the left shows the young pharaoh Tutankhamen standing on a raft. He is about to throw a harpoon. Tutankhamen lived about 1360 BC. He was king of Egypt for about 8 years and died when he was only 18 years old. The ornaments of gold and precious stones found in his tomb are the most valuable ever discovered by archaeologists. The tomb was found in 1922 by Howard Carter. It was the only tomb of a pharaoh that had not been robbed of its treasures.

Almost everything the Vikings used was covered with decoration. This included their ships. In the picture above you can see part of the carving on a Viking ship that had been made for a queen.

On the right, two Aztec women are making clothes. One is weaving on a belt-loom. It is called this because one end is attached to her by a belt. The other woman is teasing out raw cotton and spinning it into yarn.

In the East, carpets have always been important. Fine carpets, sometimes made of silk, covered the floors of palaces and mosques. Small rugs were used by people to kneel on while praying. Others were used by nomads as saddle-bags and to decorate the walls of their tents. The carpet on the right was made in Cairo in the 16th century.

INDEX

A

Abstract painting 117
Acropolis 17
Acting 110
Airbus 102
Aircraft 102–103
Albatross 62
Aleppo 24
Alexander the Great 18–19
Allah 25
Altar 16
Anak Krakatoa 81
Animals 58–59, 60–61, 72–73
Antelope 10, 59
Antennae 64
Ants 64
Apatosaurus 53
Ape-man 10
Apes 56
Arabs 24, 39
Archaeopteryx 52
Archer 36
Architecture 112
Armour 24, 25, 34–35
Art 114–115
Arthropods 65
Ash 76, 77
Aspen 76
Athena 17
Athens 16, 17
Aztecs 123

B

Bach, Johann Sebastian 120
Badger 61
Bailey 36
Ballet 118–119
Barbican 37
Bark 76
Beak 62
Beaumaris castle 36
Beaver 74–75
Beech 77
Bees 64
Beethoven, Ludwig van 121
Beetles 64
Bellflower 79
Bicycle 98
Big Boy, locomotive 97
Birch 77
Birds 62–63
Birdsfoot trefoil 79
Bistort 79
Bivalves 54, 55
Blackbird 63
Blackcap 63
Black mamba 59
Block and tackle 98
Blue butterfly 65
Blue tit 63
Blunt tellin 54
Boat 38
Boeing aircraft 102–103
Book 33
Bowsprit 42
Bradley, Janet 118
Brain 10, 100
Breastplate 34
Brick 113
Bridge 30
Bridle 69
Broad-leafed trees 76, 77
Bromine 93
Broomrape 79
Brontosaurus see Apatosaurus
Brooch 16, 29

Brunel, Isambard Kingdom 48
Bucephalus 18
Building 112, 113
Bullfinch 63
Bumblebee 61
Burial 15
Burrow 61
Burying beetle 64
Bust 121
Buttercup 79
Butterfly 64, 65
Byzantines 24, 25

C

Caliph 25
Capstan 42
Carpel 79
Carpet 123
Carter, Howard 122
Castle 36–37
Catapult 24
Caterpillar 65
Cathedral 32, 33, 112
Cats 70–71
Caveman 11
Cave painting 11
Centipede 65
Chain mail 24, 34, 36
Chalkhill blue butterfly 65
Cheetah 58, 59
Cherry tree 76
Chestnut 77
Chieftain tank 105
Chiffchaff 63
Chihuahau 67
Children 16, 46, 119
China 22–23, 27
Chisel 99
Chiton 16
Chrysalis see Pupa
Church 32, 33
Cicada 64
Citadel 24
City 21, 22, 32, 47, 106, 107
City-state 17
Clam 54
Claws 70
Clermont, steamboat 97
Cloth 46
Clothing 11, 16, 29, 114, 123
Clouded yellow butterfly 65
Clustered bellflower 79
Coat-of-mail 34
Cochlea 100
Cockle 54, 55
Cocoon 65
Coke 47
Collage 117
Collar, dog 67
Columbus, Christopher 44–45
Column 113
Compluvium 20
Composers 118, 120–121
Concorde 101, 102, 103
Concrete 112
Conifers 76, 77
Core (Earth) 88
Cowslip 79
Crack willow 77
Crafts 122–123
Crane 113
Crater 90, 91
Criollo pony 69
Crossbow 36, 116
Crow 62, 63
Crowbar 98, 99
Crusades 24, 34, 36
Crust 88, 89
Cubist painting 117
Cuisse 34
Curlew 62
Cuttlefish 54

Cutty Sark 43
Cypress 77

D

Dalmation 66
Dam, beaver 74
Dancing 25, 118–119
Dark green fritillary butterfly 65
Day 87
Deciduous trees 76
Deer 114
Deodar 77
Dinosaurs 52–53
Dionysus 110
Dogs 66–67, 114
Dog's mercury 78
Dog violet 78
Douglas fir 77
Drake, Francis 40, 41
Drawing 116
Dug-out boat 38
Dunnock 63

E

Eagle 58
Ear 62, 100
Eardrum 100
Earth 19, 42, 84, 86, 87, 88–89
Earthworm 61
Echo 100
Eclipse 84
Edinburgh castle 81
Edward I, King of England 36
Egypt 14–15, 19, 38, 39, 122
Electrical waves 100, 101
Elevation (ballet) 119
Elf owl 60
Elizabeth I 40
Elm 76, 77
Embrasure 36
Engine 48, 96–97, 102, 103
En pointe 118
Equator 88
Erectheion 16
Eric the Red 28
Evergreens 77
Exploration 40, 42, 44
Eyebright 79

F

Factory 46, 47
Falabella pony 69
Falcon 58
Farming 14, 22, 32, 47
Feathers 62
Feelers see Antennae
Ferdinand, King of Spain 44, 45
Feudalism 32
Fire 10
Flag 35
Florence 114, 115
Flowers, wild 78–79
Fly 65
Food 10, 21, 23, 42
Footplate 48
Forbidden City 27
Forecastle 42
Forum 21
Fox 61, 66
Foxglove 78
Frequency 101
Frigate bird 58
Fritillary butterfly 65
Fulton, Robert 97
Fumitory 79

G

Galleas 41
Galleon 40, 42, 43
Gastropods 54, 55
Gateway 17, 37
Gauge, railway 49

Gauntlet 34
Gazelle 59
Gears 98
Genghis Khan 26–27
Ghazi 24
Ginger cat 70
Giza 15
Glacier 89
Gold 122
Golden eagle 58
Golden Hind, The 41
Gorilla 56–57
Gothic style 112
Grands Jetés 119
Gravity 86, 94–95
Great Wall of China 22
Greave 34
Greece 16–17, 19, 38, 110–111, 112, 122
Greenfinch 63
Greenland 28
Green tit 63
Greyhound 59

H

Hadrosaurs 53
Hand, measurement 68
Hardwood trees 77
Harness 69
Hawk 62
Haydn, Joseph 121
Heath fritillary butterfly 65
Helleborine 78
Helmet 24, 34, 35
Heyerdahl, Thor 38
Hieroglyphics 15
Hill fort 17
Holly 77
Holy Land 24
Hoof 68
Horse 18, 24, 26, 35, 68–69, 114
Horse chestnut 77
Horse-collar 32
Horse markings 68
Horsepower 99
Horse racing 58, 59
Horse shoe 69
Housefly 65
House sparrow 62
Housing 20–21, 22, 23, 30, 31, 47, 112, 113
Hummingbird 58
Hunting 11, 16, 66, 67, 68, 114
Husky dog 67
Hyena 10, 66

I

Ice Age 89
Iguanadon 53
Impluvium 21
Incas 30–31
Inclined plane 98, 99
India 19, 25
Industrial Revolution 46–47
Infra-red rays 104
Insects 64–65
Internal combustion engine 96
Iron 47
Isabella, Queen of Spain 44, 45
Islam 24–25
Italy 114–115

J

Jack 98
Jackal 10, 66
Jet engine 103
Jumbo-jet 102
Jupiter 87

K

Kangaroo 72
Keel 39

Keep 36
Kestrel 62
Khafre 15
Khufu 15
Kingfisher 62
Knapweed 79
Knight 32, 34–35
Koala bear 72
Krakatoa 81
Kublai Khan 27

L
Ladybird 64
Lance 35
Larch 77
Lateen sail 39
Larva 65
Leaf 76, 77, 78
Leaf beetle 64
Leonardo da Vinci 116
Lever 98, 99
Light 100
Lime tree 76
Limpet 54, 55
Lion 70
Locomotive 48, 49, 96, 97
Lombardy poplar 76
Longbow 36
Longship 28
Long-tailed tit 63
Loom 123

M
Macedonia 18–19
Machine-gun 105
Machines 46, 98–99, 116
Magpie 63
Mail see Chain mail
Man 10–11
Mantle (Earth) 88, 89
Mantle (Shell) 54, 55
Manuscript 33
Maple 77
Marbled white butterfly 65
Marco Polo 27
Market 23
Mars 87, 107
Marsupials 72–73
Mask 110
Mauna Loa 81
Meadow brown butterfly 65
Meadow cranesbill 78
Meadow flowers 79
Medici, Lorenzo de' 114
Megalith 12
Merchant 22, 23, 32
Mercury 86
Microphone 100, 101
Middle Ages 32–37
Migration 63
Milkwort 79
Millipede 65
Mining 48
Mistle thrush 63
Moat 36
Mole 61
Molluscs 54, 55
Monastery 33
Mongolia 27
Mongols 26
Moon 90–91, 100, 106
Mortar 113
Moth 64
Motte-and-bailey 36, 37
Mozart, Wolfgang Amadeus 120
Muhammad 25
Mummy 15
Music 25, 120–121

N
Naphtha 24
Naples, Kingdom of 115

Necklace shell 54
Nelson, Admiral 42
Neptune 87
Newton, Isaac 95
New York 113
Nile river 14
Norman style 112
North Pole 88
Nutcracker 99

O
Oak 77
Oarsman 24, 38, 41
Ocean floor 92, 100
Oceans 92–93
Octopus 54
Oil painting 117
Olympic Games 16
Opossum 72
Orbit 86
Organ 120
Otter shell 54
Ovary, flower 78
Ovenbird 60
Ovule 79
Owl 60
Ox 32
Oyster 54, 55

P
Pacific Ocean 80, 92
Paddle steamer 97
Painting 33, 114, 116–117
Papyrus 14, 38
Parthenon 17
Pearl 55
Pearly nautilus 55
Pelée, Mt. 81
Peplos 16
Peregrine falcon 58
Peristyle 21
Periwinkle 55
Persia 19
Petal 78, 79
Pharaoh 15, 122
Phases of the moon 90
Philip, king of Macedonia 19
Philip II, king of Spain 40
Phobos 107
Phoenicia 38
Picasso, Pablo 117
Pine trees 76, 77
Plague 32
Plane tree 76
Planets 86
Plastering 113
Plate armour 34
Plays 110
Pluto 87
Pollination 79
Pompeii 81
Pony 68, 69
Poop 43
Poppy 79
Population 106
Pottery 122
Pouch 72–73
Power 68, 96, 99
Precious wentletrap 55
Prickly cockle 54
Primrose 79
Pulley 99, 113
Pupa 65
Pyramid 14–15

Q
Quarterdeck 43

R
Rabbit 61
Radio 100

Railway 48–49
Receptacle 78
Red clover 79
Redwood tree 76
Religion 32, 33
Renaissance 114–115
Resonance 101
Ring of Fire 80
Road 21, 30
Robin 63
Rocket, the 48
Rock painting 11
Romanesque style 112
Romans 20–21, 39, 112–113
Romulus and Remus 21
Rook 63

S
Sail 28, 39, 40–45
Sailfish 59
Salt 93
Santa Maria 44, 45
Saracen armour 34
Saturn 87
Saw 113
Scarlet pimpernel 79
Scissors 99
Scorpion 65
Scot's pine 77
Screw 99
Scribe 23
Sea anemone 59
Sea bed 92, 100
Seashells see Shells
Sea water 93
Seeds 78, 79
Sepal 78
Shallowtail butterfly 65
Sheep 46, 114
Shells 54–55
Sherman tank 104
Shetland pony 68
Shield 34
Ships 24, 38–45, 96, 123
Shire horse 68
Silver birch 77
Skyjumping 94
Skyscraper 112, 113
Slavery 14, 16, 21, 32, 114
Small copper butterfly 65
Small heath buttlerfly 65
Snail 54, 59
Snake 59
Softwood trees 77
Solar system 86
Sonar 100
Sound 100–101
Space colony 106–107
Spaceship 95, 106
Space station 107
Spain 40–41, 44
Spanish Armada 40–41
Sparrowhawk 62, 63
Speedwell 79
Spider 65
Spine-tailed swift 58, 59
Spinning 123
Spruce 77
Squid 54
Stamen 78, 79
Steam engine 46, 96–97
Steel 112
Stegosaurus 52, 53
Stephenson, George 48, 49
Step pyramid 15
Stigma 78, 79
Stonehenge 12
Stone mill 21

Stone tools 10, 11
Sun 84–87
Sunspots 84
Supersonic aircraft 102
Surtsey Island 81
Suspension bridge 30
Swallow 62, 63
Swift 58, 59
Sword 35, 37

T
Tanks 104–105
Tchaikovsky, Peter Ilyich 119
Telephone 101
Tellin 54, 55
Temple 17
Tent 35
Tent olive 55
Textile cone 55
Thatching 23
Theatre, Greek 110–111
Thoroughbred horse 68
Thrush 63
Tit 63
Toe dancing 118
Tomb 12, 15
Tools 10, 11, 14, 99, 113
Tower 23, 24, 36
Trade 22, 32, 38, 44
Trafalgar, battle of 42
Trees 76–77
Triceratops 53
Trireme 38
Turbine 96
Tutankhamen 15, 122
Tyrannosaurus 53

U
Uranus 87

V
Valhalla 29
Valley of the Kings 15
Van Gogh, Vincent 117
Varlet 36
Venice 114, 115
Venus 86, 87
Verocchio, Andrea del 116
Vesuvius, Mt. 81
Vetch 79
Vikings 28–29, 39, 123
Village 11
Volcanoes 80–81
Vulture 62

W
Walnut 77
Water 21
Water spider 60
Weaving 123
Wedge 98
Weighing 95
Weightlessness 95
Wentletrap 55
Wheel 98, 113
Wheelbarrow 98
Whelk 54, 55
Willow 77
Wing: bird 62; insect 64
Winkle 54
Wolf 66
Wood anemone 78
Woodland birds 63
Woodland flowers 78
Woodlouse 65
Woodpecker 62, 63
Woodpigeon 63
World War II 104, 105
Wren 62, 63

Z
Zeus 17